SNORKEL HAWAI'I

Maui and Lana'i

Chris Amy

Guide to the Underwater World • Judy and Mel Malinowski

Snorkel Hawai'i: Maui and Lana'i
Guide to the Underwater World

1st Edition

Published by: Indigo Publications
                 920 Los Robles Avenue
                 Palo Alto, CA 94306 USA

                 SAN 298-9921

                 Publisher's symbol: Indigo CA

First Published: 1996

Printed by: Publishers ExpressPress
                   Ladysmith, WI 54848 USA

About the cover:

Camille Young painted this lovely Hinalea (yellowtail coris) in watercolor especially for our cover. A graduate of the University of Hawai'i at O'ahu, she now lives in Moraga, California.

Dave Barry is renowned for his humorous essays and books. His love of the underwater world brings a special eloquence to these passages.

Mahalo to the kind residents of Maui and Lana'i for keeping the Aloha tradition alive, Marta Jorasch, Erland Patterson, Dave Barry, Gigi Valley, and many others.

Quotes from "Blub Story", Tropic Magazine, © Dave Barry 1989.

ISBN 0-9646680-1-7
Library of Congress Catalog Card Number: 96-095140

CONTENTS

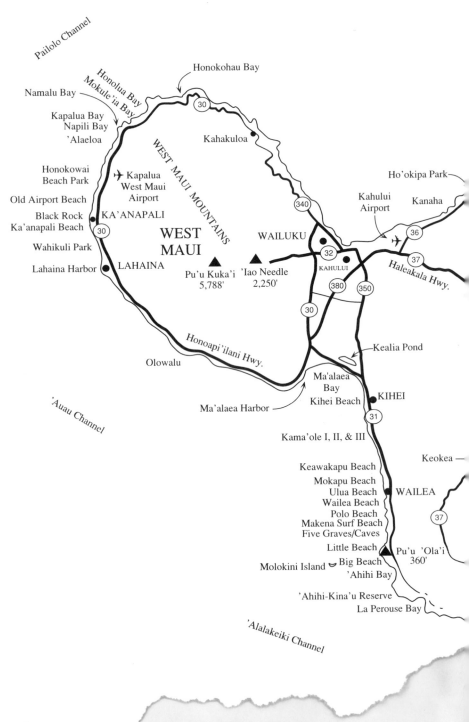

Pailolo Channel

Honokohau Bay

Namalu Bay

Honolua Bay
Mokule'ia Bay

Kapalua Bay
Napili Bay
'Alaeloa

Kahakuloa

Ho'okipa Park

Honokowai
Beach Park

Kapalua
West Maui
Airport

WEST MAUI MOUNTAINS

Kahului
Airport

Kanaha

Old Airport Beach

Black Rock
Ka'anapali Beach

KA'ANAPALI

WEST
MAUI

WAILUKU

36

Wahikuli Park

30

340

32

37

Haleakala Hwy.

Lahaina Harbor

LAHAINA

Pu'u Kuka'i
5,788'

'Iao Needle
2,250'

KAHULUI

380   350

Honoapi'ilani Hwy.

30

Olowalu

Kealia Pond

'Auau Channel

Ma'alaea
Bay
Kihei Beach

Ma'alaea Harbor

KIHEI

31

Kama'ole I, II, & III

Keokea

Keawakapu Beach

Mokapu Beach
Ulua Beach
Wailea Beach
Polo Beach
Makena Surf Beach
Five Graves/Caves

WAILEA

37

Little Beach

Molokini Island   Big Beach
'Ahihi Bay

Pu'u 'Ola'i
360'

'Ahihi-Kina'u Reserve
La Perouse Bay

'Alalakeiki Channel

MAUI

(Also see Snorkeling Site Index Map on page 42)

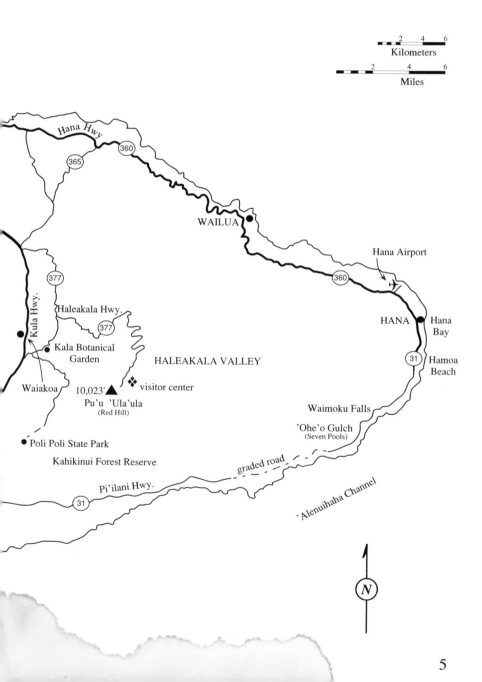

To Sophie Jorasch, Conor McGannon,
Arun and Sonia Sidhu, and Jared Gragg:
first of a new generation of snorkelers.
May they come to know and love
the underwater world as we have.

WHY MAUI?

Maui offers more snorkeling sites within easy reach than any other Hawai'ian island. There is something here for every snorkeler, and ample variety to keep a whole family happy.

Laze around on endless golden beaches and cool yourself with colorful snorkeling swims. Follow this up with good food, shopping and socializing if you're so inclined. It's all close at hand on Maui.

There are many sites with easy entry from calm, sheltered bays and broad, golden sandy beaches. Maui has extensive reefs with plenty of colorful and exciting creatures. Popular Molokini Island, with its crystal-clear waters, or the unique Island of Lana'i lie just a brief excursion away, and offer a change of pace if you're in the mood.

The choices are ample: beautiful, sweeping expanses of soft coral sand and diverse snorkeling sites; action-packed total destination resorts with all amenities; secluded little-known beach retreats just around the bend; or nearby, less touristed neighbor island hideaways. Choices like this have made Maui a legendary destination.

SNORKEL HAWAI'I MAKES IT EASY

An active vacation is memorable for adventure as well as relaxation. Hassles and missteps finding out where to go can raise your blood pressure, and waste your time. We've done extensive research that will help you quickly locate appropriate sites that fit your interests and abilities, saving your valuable vacation hours.

Snorkeling sites in Hawai'i are sometimes tricky because of changeable waves and currents, so it's best to get good advice before heading out. Everyone has had their share of unpleasant experiences due to vague directions, as well as outdated or inaccurate information. We have created the *Snorkel Hawai'i* series as that savvy snorkeling buddy everyone needs. We've included many personal stories; see *About the Authors* on page 158 if you want to know a little more about us.

We have personally snorkeled all the major sites listed. The challenge lies in knowing how to find them quickly, as well as how to enter and exit, and where to snorkel, so you'll have a safe and rewarding experience. Our detailed maps and instructions will ease the uncertainty, saving you time and effort.

Try to visit Maui and Lana'i at least once in your life, and by all means don't miss the underwater world. Aloha!

–Judy and Mel Malinowski

Snorkeling is...

- easy
- relaxing
- fun
- floating on the surface of the sea
- breathing without effort through a tube
- peering into the water world through a mask
- open to anyone of any age, size, shape or color

Who was the first snorkeler? As the fossil records include few petrified snorkels, we are free to speculate.

Among larger creatures, perhaps elephants are the pioneers and current champions, as they have known how to "snorkel" for countless generations. Once in a blue moon, you may see a elephant herd heading out to do lunch on an island off the coast of Tanzania, paddling along with their trunks held high. No one knows whether the hefty pachyderms enjoy the fish-watching, but you can bet a big liquid chuckle reverberates through the ranks of reef fish in the vicinity as the parade goes by.

As evolution continued, perhaps a clever member of the promising homo sapiens species saved his furry brow by hiding underwater from pursuers, breathing through a hollow reed. Masks came much later, so the fish probably looked a little fuzzy. Surviving to propagate his brainy kind, he founded a dynasty of snorkelers. Perhaps he actually liked the peaceful atmosphere down there, and a new sport was born.

Some of our readers may grumble that snorkeling is not a real sport: no rules, no score, no competition, scarcely aerobic, with hardly any equipment or clothing. We say to them: lighten up, you're on vacation!! Go for a long run later. Diehard competitors can create their own competition by counting how many species they've seen or trying to spot the biggest or the most seen in one day.

SCRAWLED FILEFISH

BASICS

To snorkel, you need only two things:

Snorkel	Saves lifting your head once a minute, wasting energy and disturbing the fish.
Mask	While you can see (poorly) without one, it keeps the water out of your eyes and lets you see clearly.

Rent them inexpensively at many local shops, or buy them if you prefer. It's all the back-to-basics folks need to snorkel in calm warm water, where there aren't any currents or hazards such as tidepools, your hotel pool, or your hot tub.

Savvy snorkelers often add a few things to the list, based on years of experience, such as:

Swimsuit	Required by law in many localities, possibly excluding Brazil. Added benefit: saves you from an occasional all-body sunburn.
Fins	Good if you want to swim with ease and speed, like a fish. Saves energy. A must in Hawai'i, due to occasional strong currents. They protect your tender feet, too.
T-shirt	Simple way to avoid or minimize sunburn on your back. Available everywhere in Lahaina.
Sunscreen	To slather on the tender exposed backside skin of your legs, neck, and the backs of your arms. Not optional in Hawai'i for light-skinned snorkelers.
Wetsuit	For some, the Hawai'ian waters seem a bit chilly – not exactly pool-warm. Wetsuits range from simple T-shirt-like tops to full suits. Worth considering.

You're almost ready to get wet. But wait!

You want to know even more technical detail? Just ahead, we'll go into enough detail to satisfy your deepest inner technical cravings. A major equipment shopping list if that's what you want. Every sport has an equipment list – it's what keeps sporting goods stores in business, and your garage shelves full.

GEAR SELECTION

Good snorkeling gear enables you to pay attention to the fish, instead of uncomfortable distractions. Poor equipment will make you suffer in little ways, from pressure headaches from a too-tight mask, to blisters on your feet from ill-fitting fins. Consider your alternatives carefully before buying, and you'll have more fun later.

SNORKEL

Snorkels can be quite cheap. Be prepared to pony up $15 or more if you want them to last awhile and be comfortable.

You'll appreciate a comfortable mouthpiece if you plan to snorkel for long. Watch out for hard edges – a good mouthpiece is smooth and chewy-soft.

Several new high tech models have been designed to minimize water coming down the tube from chop or an occasional swell overtopping you. We looked at these with mild skepticism until a choppy trip had us coughing and clearing our snorkels every third breath.

We took our new snorkel out to the hot tub, and tried pouring buckets of water down the tube. The snorkeler didn't even notice! Our verdict is: the new technology ones really can work as advertised. Avoid the old "float ball at the top" versions.

We use the US Divers Impulse snorkel ($35+), but others may be equally effective. An acquaintance uses and recommends a Dacor model with corrugated, flexible neck.

A bottom purge valve makes blowing out water smooth and easy, on those occasional cases when it is required. It's well worth the higher price if you snorkel in choppy water or like to surface dive.

We found that turning the "orthodontic mouthpiece" upside down on our Impulse snorkel made it more comfortable. The mouthpiece is available in two sizes, so be sure to get the one that fits your mouth. There is a company that will custom-make a mouthpiece just for you if you have a hard-to-fit mouth. Ask at your local dive shop.

You may have several colors to choose among. Although we're not especially fond of neon in clothes, bright colors can be spotted more easily in the water, and only the top of your snorkel is very visible (unless you dye your hair magenta and orange). Bright colors can also help you find dropped pieces of equipment underwater.

SNORKEL HOLDER

This little guy holds your snorkel to your mask strap, so you don't keep dipping it in the sea. The standard is a simple figure 8 double loop that pulls over the snorkel tube, wraps around your mask strap, and then back over the tube. If you are replacing one, be sure to get the right size for your tube diameter, or one that converts. Prices range from $.50 to $3. A hefty rubber band will work passably in a pinch, as well as a simple figure 8 from light cord.

An alternative high tech holder has a slot that allows the snorkel to be adjusted easily. It slides rather than having to be tugged, so is a bit easier on long hair. These come with some higher-end snorkels.

The standard Scuba snorkel position is on your left side. You might as well get used to it there, as you may dive eventually.

OCTOPUS

MASK

Nothing can color your snorkeling experience more than an ill-fitting mask. Unless, of course, you get that all-body sunburn mentioned earlier. Don't settle for painful or leaky masks! If it hurts, it's not your problem – it's the mask that's wrong for you. In this case, 'pain, no gain' applies.

Simple department store masks can cost as little as $10. Top quality ones run upwards of $60, into the low three figures in some cases, unless on sale. Consider starting out with a rental mask, paying a bit extra for the better quality models. As you build more experience, you'll be in a better position to evaluate a mask before you shell out a lot of money and lock yourself into one style.

You need a good fit to your particular face geometry. Shops often tell you to place the mask on your face (without the strap) and breathe in. If the mask will stay in place, then they say you have found a good fit. However, nearly all masks will stay on my face under this test, and yet some leak later!

Look for soft edges and a mask that conforms to your face even before drawing in your breath. There's a great deal of variance in where a mask rests on your face and how soft it feels, so compare very carefully. Look for soft and comfortable, unless you especially like having pressure headaches, or looking like a very large octopus glommed on to your face.

Good visibility is certainly important. We happen to prefer masks with glass side panels. You can't really see fish well through the side, but your peripheral vision is improved, so you can keep track of a companion without lifting your head out of the water so often.

Lack of 20-20 vision needn't cut into your viewing pleasure, but it does require a little more effort during equipment selection. Those who wear contact lenses can use them within their masks, taking on the risk that they'll swish out and float softly and invisibly down to the sea bed, perhaps to be found by a fossil hunter in the distant future, but certainly not by you. Use the disposable kind.

Vision-correcting lens are available for many masks, in 1/2 diopter increments. Unless you use contacts, search for a correctable mask. It's a real shame to finally get to those great fish, and then find them all blurry, like a TV with no antenna.

If the mask you prefer doesn't offer standard correcting lenses, custom prescription lenses can be fitted to almost any mask. This costs more and takes longer, but does produce the most accurate result. Bifocals are available. If you want these expensive options, we suggest that you water test the mask for comfort and leakage before making this extra investment.

Low volume masks

When you begin looking at masks, the variety can be bewildering. How in the world can you figure out which design is best for you?

Inexpensive masks tend to have one large flat front glass. They're OK if the skirt of the mask fits you, although they often are a bit stiff and uncomfortable. They also tend to be far out from your face, with a big air space. As you go up in price, the lenses tend to get smaller and closer to your eyes, as preferred by divers. Why is this so?

There is a good (Scuba) reason for this. These are called "low volume" masks. They contain less airspace, and so they require less effort to clear when water gets in. They also press less against your face as you go deeper, as the pressure rises (if you forget to blow higher pressure air in through your nose) and hence are more comfortable when diving.

For a snorkeler, this seems of little importance at first glance. It still should be considered as you select your mask, however, because of the possible future benefits.

Many snorkelers go on to do some surface diving, as well as Snuba or Scuba diving, and low volume is an advantage for the reasons mentioned above. When you dive down even 10', the water pressure is considerable. At 32', the air in your lungs and mask is compressed to half its volume, and unless you remember to blow some air into your mask through your nose, the pressure on your face can be most uncomfortable!

Likewise, if your mask is flooded, which does happen occasionally, it is easier to clear out the water from a low volume mask. So, while it's not the most important factor, if everything else is equal, low volume is better.

Mustaches create a mask leakage problem. As I choose to have a mustache, I have coped with this my entire adult life, excluding one amusing trip.

On a plane to Anguilla, I thought I would neatly solve the leak problem and give Judy a real surprise. I made a routine trip to the bathroom, while hiding a razor in my pocket. Off came the mustache, and then I returned, and quietly sat back down. I turned to my traveling companion, and she just about fell out of her seat! This was *not* the man she married, and she had the odd experience of feeling like she was vacationing with a stranger. The verdict: she preferred her familiar old companion. Mustache mask leaks are better than marital discord.

There are those who use petroleum jelly to make a more effective seal. That doesn't appeal to me, going in and out of the water twice or more a day. It does help to choose a mask that rests high over the mouth and perhaps trim the top 1/8" or so of the center mustache, if it sticks up. Hair breaks the seal and allows water to seep into the mask slowly, so you'll still have to clear the mask occasionally.

Anyone with a leaky mask may prefer having a purge valve. There are some clever higher-end purge valve masks. The conventional wisdom in Scuba is that purge valves are an unnecessary weak point. Nevertheless, there are experienced divers who use them regularly without having any problems.

A purge valve can quickly and cheaply be added to some masks, by some dive shops (if you have a bit of space just under the nose of your mask), but it is a bit less fail safe for diving. You can also compensate by tightening the mask, but that's not particularly comfortable and leaves a distinct mask mark on your face at the end of the snorkeling day, as if a giant octopus tentacle has been sucking on your face.

MASK STRAP

The strap that comes with the mask is generally fine, but if you have your own mask and want it to slide on more easily, there's a comfortable strap available with adjustment by velcro. The back is made of wetsuit material, stretchy and soft. They supposedly will float if your mask should come off, but ours don't. A big benefit: no more hair tangles in the strap! Cost: about $12 in dive shops, but they're not always easy to find. Since we get in and out so often, we happen to prefer this one to a rubber strap, but it's a convenience for the frequent snorkeler, rather than a necessity.

FINS

The simplest fins are basic (usually black) enclosed foot fins. These are one-piece molded rubber, and slip right on to your bare feet. For warm water, basic snorkeling, these inexpensive fins are fine. We own several kinds of fins, and still often choose the one-piece rubber foot fins for lightness and easy packing. They seem to last forever ($15–$25).

Why should anyone look further? Well, specialized fins are now made for special uses, and higher performance. We recently performance tested three sets of fins, doing timed swims over a measured course. The basic fins discussed above went first. A set of fairly expensive, but rather soft, flexible strap-on fins cut the swim time by 20%, while ultra long, stiff-bladed foot-mount Cressi fins cut it by 40%! These long surface diving fins are, however, a little long and awkward to use for most surface snorkeling or even Scuba.

There is a vigorous debate going on among divers about the merits of flexible fin blades versus stiff blades. We've tested both, and our opinion is that the most efficient are light, thin, stiff blades, hands down. We have a pair of top quality, but soft blade fins we'd just love to sell to you, cheap, if you are of a different opinion.

You're better off with a medium blade size foot fin for most snorkeling. Large diving fins are awkward for snorkeling, and require more leg strength than most non-athletes possess. The big diving fins do come in numerous shapes and colors, which some people are convinced will make them faster or perhaps more attractive. Speed is not the main aim of snorkeling, but has its uses.

Faster fins do enable you to cover more territory, and they also serve as excellent insurance in case you wander into a strong current. Unless it's absolutely certain that no current can carry you away, ALWAYS WEAR FINS!

MILLETSEED
BUTTERFLYFISH

As you look at more advanced fins, they split into two attachment methods, with pros and cons to each type. We own both, and pick the best for a particular situation. Some models are available in both attachment styles.

ENCLOSED FOOT   Your bare foot slides into a stretchy, integral molded rubber 'shoe'.

Advantages   This gives the lightest, most streamlined and fish-like fit. It probably is the most efficient at transmitting your muscle power to the blade. We like these best when booties are not required for warmth or safety.

Disadvantages   The fins must be closely fitted to your particular foot size. Some models may rub your skin wrong, creating blisters. If you have to hike in to the entry site, you need separate shoes. This may preclude entering at one spot, and exiting elsewhere. If you hike over rough ground (lava, for example) to get to your entry point, or the entry is over sharp coral or other hazards, these may not be the best choice.

STRAP-ON   Made for use with booties.

Advantages   Makes rough surface entry easy. Just hike to the entry point, head on into the water holding your fins in hand, lay back and pull on your fins. Exiting is just as easy. The bootie cushions your foot, making blisters unlikely. Widely used for Scuba.

Disadvantages   Less streamlined. The bootie makes your foot float up, so you may have trouble keeping your fins from breaking the surface at times. Some divers use ankle weights to counter this, but they can tire you, and slow you down.

REEF SHOES OR BOOTIES

Walking with bare feet on lava or coral can shred your feet in a quick minute. There are fine reef shoes available that are happy in or out of the water. These are primarily for getting there, or wading around, as they don't really work that well with strap-on fins. For the sake of the reef, don't actually walk on a reef with them, as each step kills hundreds of the little animals that make up the living reef.

Zip-on booties are widely used by divers, and allow use of strap-on fins. They do float your feet up some, a minor annoyance for snorkelers. Some divers use ankle weights to counter this.

Judy prefers her small enclosed foot fins, so she carries along cheap old shoes or reef shoes to cross a rough area, and then just leaves them at the entry point. Use old, grungy ones no one would want to steal. In Hawai'i lots of shops and markets sell reasonably priced versions of reef shoes, which are very handy if you like to explore.

CONVICT TANG

KEEPING TIME

One easy-to-forget item: a water-resistant watch. This needn't be expensive, and is very useful. It's essential for pacing yourself, and keeping track of your sun exposure time. We prefer a slim, analog watch with a nice clean uncluttered face and easy to read numbers. Inexpensive simple Timex water-resistant watches have given us good performance, up until it's time to change the battery!

"Water resistant" alone usually means that a little rain won't wreck the watch, but immersion in water may. When "to 50 meters" is added, it denotes added water-resistance; but the dynamic pressures from swimming increase the pressure, so choose 50 meters or greater rating to be safe even when snorkeling. It does help to not press any of the buttons while you are underwater. Don't take a 50 meter watch Scuba diving, though – that requires 100-200 meter models.

Hawai'ian time is two hours earlier than Pacific Standard Time, or three hours earlier than Pacific Daylight Time. Hawai'i doesn't observe Daylight Savings Time.

BODY SUITS

There are a variety of all-body suits that protect you from sun exposure and light abrasion, but provide little warmth. They are made from various synthetic fabrics, lycra and nylon being common. They cost less than wetsuits, and are light and easy to pack. These are more effective at warding off sunburn than T-shirts, and are also good for midday windsurfing or sailing. We often carry ours in case the water and weather are especially warm, but we'd prefer not getting nipped by bothersome jellyfish or little floating bits of hydroids that occasionally show up in numbers.

WETSUIT

Water temperature on the surface varies from a low of about 77° F in March to a high of about 80° in September. If you happen to be slender, no longer young and from a moderate climate, this can seem cold. Sheltered bays and tidepools can be a bit warmer, while deeper water can be surprisingly cold. We've snorkeled in March when we swore it was not above 65° off Kaua'i.

Regardless of the exact temperature, the water is cooler than your body. With normal exertion, your body still cools, bit by bit. After awhile, perhaps 30-45 minutes, you start feeling a little chilly. Later, you begin shivering, and then eventually, hypothermia begins.

A wetsuit isn't necessary in Hawai'i, but it sure makes being in the water a lot more fun for many who are slim or who have a lower metabolism. We like to snorkel for two hours or more, and a thin wetsuit protects us from the sun, while keeping us warm and comfortable as well.

Off the rack suits are a bargain, and fit many folks. We have seen Costco carrying perfectly adequate shortie (short sleeve arms and above-the-knee legs) suits for under $60. Look for a snug fit at neck, arms and legs – if your suit is loose there, water will flow in and out, making you cold. If you have big feet and small ankles, get zippers on the legs if possible if you decide to buy a full length suit.

PARROTFISH

We are both tall and skinny, so off-the-shelf suits don't fit well. Our standby suit is a light, full body custom-made suit, with 3mm body, and 2mm arms and legs. Judy had zippers installed on both arms and legs. After we got these suits, our pleasure level while snorkeling in Hawai'i went way up. They also suffice for most warm-water diving situations.

Wetsuit wearers also get added *range*. Wearing a wetsuit, you can stay in the water without hypothermia for many hours. This could be comforting in the unlikely event that some strong current sweeps you off towards Fiji. There are few situations that you cannot rescue yourself from if you have a wetsuit and fins.

SWIM CAP

If you have trouble with long hair tangling in your gear while snorkeling, a Speedo swim cap can help. Women who swim regularly for exercise use them to cut hair wear and tear.

A cap is particularly useful if you're entering the water multiple times per day, since wet, salty hair has a perverse way of weaving itself into the buckles and straps of your mask. Look for swim caps in any large sporting goods store.

SNORKELING VEST

It is possible to buy inflatable vests made for snorkeling. Some guidebooks and stores promote them as virtually essential. We've even been on excursion boats that require all snorkelers to wear one.

Use your own judgement, with prudence erring on the side of caution, of course. We're not convinced, however, that vests are essential, or even the best alternative.

Vests are hardly necessary in salt water for most people, but can be useful if you can't swim a lick or won't be willing to try this sport without it. There is a possible safety edge for kids or older folks. If you do get a vest, you can give it to another beginner after you get used to snorkeling. You'll have discovered that it takes almost no effort to float flat in the water while breathing through a snorkel.

If you want extra flotation, consider using a light wetsuit instead. It simultaneously gives you a little more buoyancy, sun and critter protection, and warmth too!

SURFACE DIVING GEAR

For surface diving, bigger fins help your range. Those surreal-looking Cressi fins that seem about three feet long will take you down so fast you'll be amazed.

Be careful down there, though. Periodically, you read about yet another expert surface-diver who passed the oxygen deprivation edge, blacked out and drowned. If you like living more than danger, don't push your limits too far. With a little good judgement and technique, surface diving can be both fun and safe.

A long-fin alternative is to use a weight belt with from 2-4 pounds – just enough to help you get under the surface without using up all your energy. As you descend, you become neutrally buoyant at about 15-20' so you don't have to fight popping up. Of course, the sword cuts two ways, as you must swim up under your own power in time to breathe!

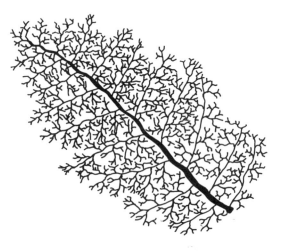

INTO THE WATER

GETTING STARTED

Now you've assembled a nice collection of snorkel gear. You're ready to go! On a sunny tropical morning you have walked down to the water's edge. Little one-foot waves slap the sand lightly, while a soft warm breeze takes the edge off the intensity of the climbing sun. It's a great day to be alive, and out in the water.

Since you're going snorkeling, you've refrained from applying suntan lotion on your face. You sure don't want it washing into your eyes, to make them burn and water. You've worn a nice big hat instead. You applied lotion to your back before you left, so it had time to become effective. Then you washed off your hands and rinsed them well so the lotion couldn't contaminate your mask later.

CHECKING CONDITIONS

Take it nice and slow, one thing at a time. Sit down and watch the waves for a few minutes. Look for their patterns, how big the biggest waves are, and how far they wash up on the beach. When you see the pattern, you're ready to go. Set your gear down back beyond where the furthest watermarks are on the sand. You don't want that seventh wave to sweep your gear away!

GEARING UP

Take your mask in hand, and defog it. You treat the lens so that water vapor from your nose, or water leakage, won't bead up on your mask lens and spoil your view. There are two main chemical compounds for this, one old as us, and the other a product of modern chemistry.

The classic solution is: SPIT. Spit on the inside of your dry mask lens, and rub it all around with your sunscreen-free finger. Step into the water, just out beyond the stirred up sand, and dip up a mask full of clear saltwater. Thoroughly rub and rinse off that spit, and dump the mask. Now you have prepared a mask that should be fog-resistant for an average snorkel!

If you spit and polish, and still have fogging problems, there are several possible causes. Your mask may be gooped up with cosmetics, dried on saltwater residue, or whatever other goos may be out there. A good cleaning with toothpaste may be in order (*see Caring for Your Gear, page 29*). It's possible that you didn't actually wet all the surface with spit, perhaps because there were drops of water left on the lens.

Of course, you may be spit-deficient, which government studies have determined occurs in 14% of the snorkeling population. Tough break. In that case, or if you just feel funny about spitting in your mask, you can use no-fog solution.

No-fog solution for masks actually *does* work even better than spit. It comes in small, handy, inexpensive bottles that seem to last forever, because you use only a few drops at a time.

Our favorite trick is to pre-apply no-fog to the dry masks an hour or more ahead, and let it dry on. When you get to the water, just rinse out thoroughly, and you get even better results!

MOORISH IDOL

GETTING COMFORTABLE

After you rinse your mask, try its fit. Adjust the mask strap and snorkel until they're quite comfortable. Hold the snorkel in your mouth without tightening your jaws. It can be quite loose and will not fall out.

When you like the fit, pull it down over your head so it rests on your forehead or chest. In some Scuba circles, putting your mask up on your forehead is a signal of distress, so it will make some divers nervous if you do it. We don't find this rule convincing, at least for snorkelers. Your forehead is about the most practical mask storage place. Putting your mask on long before you enter the water can cause it to fog from your exertions.

GETTING WET

Now retrieve your fins and walk back in the water, watching the waves carefully. NEVER turn your back on the ocean for long, lest a rogue wave sneak up on you and whack you good. The key is to stay alert and awake, remembering that you are the one in charge here.

If the bottom is sandy smooth, wade on out until you're about waist deep. Pull your mask on, making sure you remove any stray hair from under the skirt. Position the snorkel in your mouth, and start breathing. You can practice this back in your room, or even at a pool or in the hot tub if you like acting wild and crazy. Not too crazy – don't snorkel under the influence!

Duck down in the water so you're floating, and pull on your flippers just like sneakers. Make a smooth turn to your stomach, pause to float and relax until you're comfortable, and you're off! Flip those fins, and you have begun your re-entry into the sea.

As you float, practice steady, even breathing through the snorkel. Breathe slowly and deeply. People sometimes tense up at first and take short breaths. When this happens, you're only getting stale air from the snorkel rather than lots of fresh air from outside. If you ever feel tired or out of breath, don't take off your mask and snorkel. Just stop for several minutes, float, breathe easy, and relax.

After you've become quite comfortable breathing this way, check how your mask is doing. Make sure it isn't leaking. Have your buddy check it out also. Adjust the strap if needed. And keep adjusting until it's just right. Slide your snorkel strap to a comfortable position, with the tube pointing about straight up as you float looking down at about a 30° angle. This is a good time to remove any sand that got in your flippers.

Swimming while snorkeling is quite easy once you've relaxed (*see Snorkeling is easier than swimming, page 25*). No arms are required. What works best is to hold your arms straight and smooth back along your sides, keep your legs fairly straight and kick those fins slowly without bending your knees. Any swimming technique will work, of course, but some are more tiring. Practice using the least amount of energy just to make sure you can do it. Once you learn how to snorkel the easy way, you can use all the power you like touring large areas as if you were a migrating whale.

Snorkeling is easier than swimming

Some folks never learn to snorkel because they're not confident as swimmers. This is an unnecessary loss, because snorkeling is actually easier than swimming. We have maintained this to friends for years, and noted their doubtful looks. Recently, we came across a program in California that actually uses snorkeling as a tool to help teach swimming!

The Transpersonal Swimming Institute in Berkeley, CA specializes in the teaching of adults who are afraid of the water. Local heated pools are used all year. But the warm, salty and buoyant ocean is the best pool of all.

Melon Dash, Director of TSI, takes groups of her students to Hawai'i 5-7 times a year. They begin by floating comfortably in the warm, salty Hawai'ian water. At their own pace, they gradually learn to snorkel, and be comfortable in the water.

"We have found that people cannot learn what to do with their arms and legs while they are afraid that they might not live."

With a steady air supply, not having to worry about breathing in water accidentally, they can relax and learn the arm and leg movements at ease. Happily, they soon discover there's nothing complicated about it!

In calm conditions, with warm water, there need be no age limits and few physical limits for snorkeling. Some lap swimmers prefer to swim with mask and snorkel, as they get a full, easy air supply that way, and no chlorine in their eyes.

Transpersonal Swimming Institute
P.O. Box 2254
Berkeley, CA 94702-0054

Outside CA (800) 723-7946
(510) 526-6000
fax (510) 526-6091
Transwim@aol.com

CLEARING YOUR MASK

Eventually you will need to practice clearing your mask of water that leaks into it. The Scuba method: Take a deep breath, then tip your head up, but with the mask still just under the surface. Press your palm to the top of the mask against your forehead, or hold your fingers on the top of the mask while lightly easing pressure on the bottom of the mask, and exhale through your nose. This forces the water out the bottom of the mask. You may need to do this more than once to get all the water out.

Lifting your head out of the water and releasing the seal under your nose will work too, but is frowned on by dive instructors, because it won't work under water. They would hate to see you develop bad habits if there's any chance you'll take up diving later. It also uses up more energy and is harder in choppy conditions.

TAKING IT EASY

Relax and try not to push yourself too hard. Experienced snorkelers may urge you on faster than you're comfortable because they've forgotten how it feels to get started. As your experience builds, you'll find it easy too.

It's a bit like learning to drive a car. Remember how even a parking lot seemed like a challenge? It helps to practice your beginning snorkeling in a calm easy place – with a patient teacher. With a little persistence, you'll soon overcome your fears and be ready. Don't feel like you should rush. Just play around and have fun. If you're having a slow start, try snorkeling in the shallow end of your hotel pool.

KNOWING YOUR LIMITS

Have you heard the old saloon saying: "Don't let your mouth write checks that your body can't cover"?

Let's paraphrase this as "Don't let your ego take you places your body can't get you back from." Consider carefully how well-conditioned your legs are, so you'll have enough reserve to be able to make it back home, and then some in case of an emergency.

SNORKELING ALONE

In your enthusiasm for the reef, you may wind up in this situation: your significant other prefers watching sports on ESPN to snorkeling one afternoon, and you're sorely tempted to just head out there alone.

DON'T DO IT. Think about it hard, face the temptation, swallow hard, and just say no. Your descendants will thank you.

Snorkeling, done in buddy teams, is a pretty safe recreation, especially if conditions are favorable. Just as in Scuba diving, having a buddy along reduces the risk of a small problem becoming a big problem, or even a fatal problem.

Snorkeling done alone increases the risks. We won't spell out all the bad things that could happen; we trust your imagination. The risks are small, but the consequences can be large.

If you have connections in high places that exempts you from these risks and, ignoring our prudent advice, you do go out alone, try to at least limit yourself to well-protected sites under good conditions, and stay near other swimmers and snorkelers. Remember, though, that they have no particular reason to pay attention to you, and may disappear without notice, leaving you on your own.

Pacing

When you're having a good time, it's easy to forget and overextend yourself. That next rocky point beckons, and then a pretty spot beyond that. Pretty soon, you're many miles from home, and getting cold and tired. Getting overly tired can contribute to poor judgement in critical situations, making you more vulnerable to injury. Why risk turning your great snorkeling experience into a pain? Learn your limits, and how to pace yourself.

Our favorite technique: If we plan on a 1 hour snorkel, we watch the time, and start heading back when we've swum 30 minutes. If the currents could run against us on the way back, we allow extra time/energy.

BOTTLENOSED DOLPHIN

SPINNER DOLPHINS

CARING FOR YOUR GEAR

You just had a great snorkeling experience – now you can thank the gear that helped make it possible, by taking good care of it.

RINSE AND DRY

If there are beach showers, head right up and rinse off. Salt residue is sticky and corrosive. Rinse it and any sand off your wetsuit, fins, mask, snorkel, and any other gear before the saltwater dries on.

If you can, dry your gear in the shade. It's amazing how much damage sun can do to the more delicate equipment – especially the mask. When the sun odometer hits 100,000 miles, you can kiss those rubber parts goodbye.

SAFETY INSPECTIONS

Keep an eye on vulnerable parts after a few years (strap, snorkel-holder, buckles). Parts are usually easy to find in Hawai'i, but not in the middle of a snorkeling trip unless you're on a well-equipped boat. We've snorkeled for an hour with one fin after an aging strap gave way, just as it was stretched too far in the process of gearing up.

If you use any equipment with purge valves, keep an eye on the delicate little flap valves, and replace them when they deteriorate.

Inspect your stretch suit or wetsuit for weakening seams, or the beginnings of splits and tears. You're stretching this gear every time you put it on, and it cannot last forever.

Look out for water droplets on the inside of your watch lens. Once saltwater gets in, battery failure soon follows. Sometimes, baking the watch in the sun to drive out the moisture may turn the trick, and the watch will keep working. If you have a battery replaced, ask if the shop can also replace the o-ring gasket. This will improve your chances of staying water-tight.

CLEAN YOUR MASK

A mask needs a thorough cleaning between trips as well. Use a regular, non-gel toothpaste to clean the lens inside and out, polishing off accumulated goo. There's no point in going all this way to look at fascinating creatures through little dried-on spots on the lens. Wash the toothpaste off with warm water, using your finger to clean it well.

HAZARDS

Life is just not safe. If you go out for a walk, it's possible that a
meteor will fall from the sky and bonk you on the head,
occasionally. If that can happen, it stands to reason that snorkeling
may have a few hazards that you should know and avoid if possible.

Obviously you already know the dangers of car and air travel, yet
you mustered your courage and decided that a trip to Hawai'i was
worth the risks. And you took reasonable precautions, like buckling
your seat belt. Well, if you use your noggin, you're probably safer
once in the water than you are driving to get *to* the water.

Some people are hesitant to snorkel because they imagine meeting a
scary creature in the water. But it's actually safer to see them than to
be swimming over them not knowing what's there.

We don't think it makes sense to overemphasize certain lurid
dangers (sharks!) and pay no attention to the more likely hazards of
sunburn and stepping on sea urchins (which certainly cause far
more aggravation to large numbers of tourists).

Risks are always relative and we often react emotionally rather than
rationally at the thought of them. On a tranquil Caribbean isle, an
old woman warned us to *be careful!* because of all the murders
there. She was eager to tell all the details. Three local people had
been killed by their spouses. She then assured us these heinous
crimes had all taken place within just the last one hundred years!

SUNBURN

Undoubtedly the worst medical problem you're likely to face,
especially if you have the wrong ancestors. Use extra water-resistant
sunblock in the water and always wear a shirt during the day. Some
people need to avoid the sun entirely from 10:00 to 3:00, but that's a
good excuse to go early and avoid the crowds. The top (or open)
deck of a boat is a serious hazard to the easily-burned. The best
protection is covering up, as evidence mounts that sunscreen still
allows skin damage, even though it stops burning.

Sunlight penetrates the water. It also reflects extremely well from
water and white sand. In Australia, high skin cancer rates believed
due in part to a hole in the ozone layer have heightened awareness
of the dangers of reflected sunlight. Kids are being taught to wear
light hats with a dark under-brim, as well as dark shirts, to avoid
reflecting more rays onto their faces.

It's better not to have sunscreen on your face or hands when putting on your mask, though, because you'll be sorry later when your mask leaks a bit and you get the stuff in your eyes. It can really burn and even make it difficult to see well enough to navigate back to shore.

To avoid using gallons of sunblock, some snorkelers wear lycra body suits. Others simply wear some old clothing, even button-down shirts or old khakis. Loose knits don't work as well because they often balloon out under water – making it tricky to swim.

A few old pro tips: Take an old sun hat to leave on the beach, especially if you have to hike midday across a reflective white beach. Take old sunglasses that are not theft-worthy. If you must leave prescription glasses on the beach, use your old ones. Maui is a great place to find amazingly cheap ($2) sunglasses and flip-flops. For your longer hours in the sun, look into the better sunglasses that carefully filter all the most damaging rays.

RIP CURRENTS

Hawai'i does not have large barrier reefs to intercept incoming waves. Few of Maui's beaches are well-protected from powerful ocean currents – especially in the winter or during storms.

Waves breaking against a shore push volumes of water up close to the shore. As this piles up, it has to flow back to the ocean, and often flows sideways along the shore until it reaches a convenient, often deeper bottomed, exit point. There, a fast, narrow river of water flows out at high speed. Rip currents, which can carry swimmers out quickly, are usually of limited duration, by their very nature, and usually stop no more than 100 yards out.

Sometimes it's possible to swim sideways, but often it's better to simply ride it out. Don't panic. Although the current might be very strong, it won't take you far or drown you, unless you exhaust yourself by swimming against it. It's very easy to float in salt water until help arrives, assuming you're at a beach where someone can see you. Don't try to swim in through waves where there's any chance of being mashed on lava rocks or coral. Don't swim against the current to the point of exhaustion. When in doubt, float and conserve energy.

Even at the most protected beaches (like Kapalua Bay), all the water coming in must get out, so there's a current somewhere. Big waves beyond the breakwater may seem harmless, but the more water comes in, the more must get out. This is a good reason to ALWAYS wear fins.

HYPOTHERMIA

Open ocean water is always cooler than your body, and it cools you off more rapidly than the air. With normal exertion, your body still cools, bit by bit. After awhile, perhaps 30-45 minutes for most folks, you start feeling a little chilly. Later, you begin shivering, and then eventually hypothermia begins. When your body temperature has dropped enough, your abilities to move and even think begin to get impaired. If your temperature drops too low, you eventually die.

One of the first symptoms of hypothermia is poor judgement. Swimmers and snorkelers can watch out for each other better than you can watch out for yourself alone – one example of the benefits of having a partner. Check up on each other often in cold conditions.

As soon as you are aware that you're cold, it's time to plan your way back. When shivering starts, you should get out of the water ASAP! Be particularly careful in situations requiring all your judgement and skill to be safe, especially when diving, night snorkeling, dealing with waves, or when anticipating a difficult exit from the water.

Usually it's quite easy to warm up rapidly since the air temperature is fairly warm at sea level. A person suffering from hypothermia cannot warm up without help. Even without hypothermia, it's good to warm up between snorkels. If you came by car, it is usually well solar-heated by the time you return, and will help you warm up.

SEA URCHINS

Probably the most common critter injury is stepping on a spiny sea urchin, and walking away with lots of spines under your skin. The purple-black ones with long spines tend to appear in groups and favor shallow water, so watch carefully if you see even one. Full-foot flippers or booties help a lot, but don't guarantee protection. Watch where you put your hands – especially in shallow water.

While many folks recommend seeing a doctor for urchin spine slivers, others prefer to just let the spines fester and pop out weeks later. Read *The Snows of Kilimanjaro* one more time before trying this self-treatment. You don't want a killer infection setting in.

Remove as much spine as you can, though it's impossible to remove it all. Vinegar (or other acidic liquid) will make it feel better. Periodic soaking in Epsom salts helps, and the small spines will dissolve in a few weeks. See a doctor at any sign of infection. The area will likely turn purple from the dye in the spines, but that will gradually disappear.

Waves are travelling ripples in the water, mostly generated by wind blowing over large expanses of water. Having energy, the waves keep going until something stops them, and may travel thousands of miles before dissipating that energy. Here is the wellspring of the breaking surf. That beautiful surf can also be the biggest danger facing snorkelers.

Take time occasionally to sit on a high point and watch the waves approaching the coast, and you will see patterns emerge. Usually there is an underlying groundswell from one direction, waves that may have originated in distant storms. This is the main source of the rhythmical breaking waves, rising and falling in size in noticeable patterns. Often, there will be a series of small waves, and then one or more larger waves, and the cycle repeats. Pay attention to the patterns and it will be less likely that you'll get caught by surprise.

Local winds add their own extra energy, in their own directions. In Hawai'i, snorkeling is usually easiest in the mornings, before the daily winds build and make larger waves in the afternoon. Many excursions head out early to make sure they have smooth sailing and calm snorkeling.

Occasionally, a set of larger waves or a single large *rogue* wave comes in with little or no warning. A spot that was protected by an offshore reef suddenly has breaking waves. This is a problem that shouldn't be underestimated.

Our single worst moment in many years of snorkeling and diving was at Brenneke's Beach in Kaua'i after Hurricane Iniki had scattered boulders throughout the beach. We had no problem snorkeling around the boulders in a light swell, protected by reef further out. Suddenly much larger waves crossed the reef and began breaking over us, sweeping us back and forth. Judy was swept into some boulders, leaving bruises on elbows, knees and hip. Fortunately, her wetsuit cushioned the blows enough that no bones were broken.

Since then we have been extra careful to avoid hazardous situations. We always take time to study the waves before entering and ponder what would happen if they suddenly grew much larger, and what our strategy would be. Sometimes we just head for a calmer beach.

BARRACUDA

The Great Barracuda can grow to two meters, has sharp teeth and strong jaws, and swims like a supercharged torpedo. For years Judy has removed earrings before swimming after hearing rumors that they attract barracuda, but we've uncovered absolutely no confirming reports of severed ears.

GREAT BARRACUDA

Barracuda can, if motivated, seriously injure a swimmer, and should be taken seriously. Those teeth are just as sharp as they look. Even small barracuda can be aggressive, so don't bother them in any way. They look like they have attitude, and apparently sometimes do.

Our own preference is to respect their territory and don't push or pursue them. Many divers just don't worry about them a bit, and actively seek them out.

Other varieties of barracuda, such as the Heller's that you see at 'Ahihi, *appear* more innocuous. Barracuda are not very common in Hawai'i anyway, and you'll probably count yourself lucky to see one.

Once a five foot Great Barracuda swam directly beneath our party of four snorkelers in the Caribbean and appeared annoyed that we were invading his home territory (or so we thought from the fierce look on his face). A calm and steady German surgeon headed up the nearest rocks as if she could fly. The rest of us snorkeled by him repeatedly with no problem, but didn't appreciate the look he gave us. We later came to realize that they always look grumpy, but seldom bite, like some folks you may know.

PORTUGUESE MAN-O'WAR

The Portuguese Man-o'War floats on top, looking like a sailfin 1"-4" in size, with long stinging filaments that are quite painful. Stay out of the water if you see one. Even avoid dead ones on the sand! They stay on top of the water with an air-filled bladder and can unroll their long filaments. They're very pretty – shades of purple, but can cause severe pain. Sometimes you don't even see anything, but just feel the sting and see long red lines on your body. When Mel encountered one, he felt a whip-like sting on his arm, and a curving red welt appeared. Ouch!

Vinegar and unseasoned meat tenderizer helps ease the sting and helps stop the release of venom from the stinging cells if tentacles are clinging to you. Use wet sand as a last resort. If you feel very ill, see a doctor right away. Other jellyfish can often be completely harmless. If jellyfish are present, locals will know which ones are a problem. Jellyfish have not been a big problem for us in Hawai'i.

RAYS

Sting rays prefer to avoid you, but hang out on the bottom where they're easy to step on. They prefer resting in calm water that is slightly warmer than the surrounding area – which are just the areas favored by people for swimming. Step on them and they may sting you, so the injury is usually to the foot or ankle. They can inflict a serious or painful sting to people – especially children. It's best to get immediate first aid and follow up with medical assistance.

Snorkelers have an advantage in this case over swimmers because snorkelers can see rays and easily avoid them. In Maui we've seen them swim between children's legs in shallow water at Kapalua Bay and were amazed to see how adept they were at avoiding people when they are free to do so.

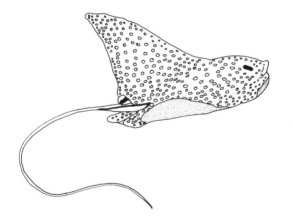

SPOTTED
EAGLE RAY

Manta rays don't sting although they're much larger. Of course, they can be bigger than you are, so they certainly can knock you over if you get in their way. Around Maui they are often seen six to eight feet across, weighing several hundred pounds, and can get even larger. They maneuver beautifully, so there isn't much danger unless you're a terrible klutz. Divers though have to be a bit more careful to not have their equipment knocked off inadvertently.

Any serious snorkeler should bother to learn some basic signs starting with some of the standard Scuba ones: OK – meaning "Are you OK?", which should be answered with another "OK", palm up for "stop", wobbling hand for "problem", thumb down meaning "heading down" (in this case referring to surface diving). This is an essential safety issue making it possible to communicate even if slightly separated. See signs below.

It's also a nuisance to take the snorkel out of your mouth every time you want to say "Did you see that moray?" Worse yet is trying to understand your buddy who frantically gestures and mumbles through the snorkel while you play charades. With a frequent snorkeling companion it's fun to develop signs for the creatures you might see. Eel can be indicated by three fingers looking like an E or by a wavy line drawn in the water. Then all you have to do it point and there it is!

Learning actual ASL sign language could be a plus – although there aren't too many fish or marine life signs yet, and spelling letter by letter is slow unless you're both accomplished signers.

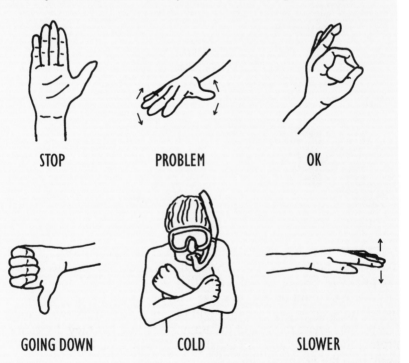

STOP   PROBLEM   OK

GOING DOWN   COLD   SLOWER

POISONOUS FISH

Lionfish (also called turkeyfish) and scorpionfish have spines which are very poisonous. Don't step on or touch them! Their poison can cause serious pain and infection or allergic reaction, so definitely see a doctor if you have a close, personal encounter with one. Better yet, don't! Flippers or booties can help protect your tender feet.

Scorpionfish can blend in so well along the bottom in shallow water that they're easy to miss. Turkeyfish, though, are colorful and easy to spot. Since these fish are not abundant, they are treasured sightings.

TURKEYFISH
(LIONFISH)

EELS

Eels are rarely aggressive, and are often tamed by divers. They do possess a formidable array of teeth, which should be avoided. No one would intentionally stick their hand into a hole in the reef to aggravate an eel with those sharp teeth and strong jaws. However, it's easy for the currents and swell to bring you right up close to an eel, surprising you both.

If you are bitten, it's supposedly better to wait till he lets you go, rather than trying to rip yourself away. If you have any personal experience, write us with details. We haven't yet met an actual eel bite victim.

LEOPARD MORAY EEL

An eel bite can definitely cause serious bleeding requiring prompt medical attention. A good reason not to snorkel alone! Snorkelers see plenty of eels in Hawai'i, and they are easy to find and fascinating. Count on eels to make every effort to avoid you, so there's no need to panic at the sight of one – even if it's swimming freely. Eels aren't interested in humans as food, but they do want to protect themselves and can usually do so with ease by slipping away into the nearest hole.

CONE SHELLS

The snails inside these pretty black and brown-decorated shells can fire a poisonous dart. The venom can cause a serious reaction or even death – especially to allergic persons. If in doubt, head for a doctor. This can be easily avoided by not picking up underwater shells in the first place.

SHARKS

Sharks are seldom a problem for snorkelers. In Hawai'i the modest number of verified shark attacks have mostly occurred off O'ahu, with tiger sharks the major perpetrator. As sharks often hunt in very murky river runoff, eating shellfish and whatever else washes down, there is extra risk swimming in times of high runoff. Of course, those are not conditions you're likely to snorkel in, anyway.

Some people will suggest you can pet, feed or even tease certain types of shark. I personally would give sharks a bit of respect and leave them entirely in peace. Most sharks are well-fed on fish, and not all that interested in oiled tourists, but it's hard to tell by looking at a shark whether it has had a bad day. Sharks are territorial, so they can be more aggressive on a first encounter. They especially feed late in the day or at night, causing some people to prefer to enjoy the water more in the morning or midday. If you're in an area frequented by sharks, this might be good to keep in mind.

In Hawai'i divers can see sandbar, black tip and Galapagos sharks. Sandbar sharks will usually swim off quickly, but others might be curious or unconcerned.

In spite of what folks say, any shark that is 2' or larger could bite you in the right circumstances. Get out of the water if they start hanging around or seem excessively curious. Stay perfectly still, or swim steadily away, rather than thrashing around and doing an imitation of a wounded animal.

REEF SHARK

38

I like to watch

"For some reason, the barracuda don't seem scary, any more than the ray does. For some reason, none of this seems scary. Even the idea of maybe encountering a smallish s___k doesn't seem altogether bad.

It's beginning to dawn on me that all the fish and eels and crabs and shrimps and plankton who live and work down here are just too busy to be thinking about me.

I'm a traveller from another dimension, not really a part of their already event-filled world, not programmed one way or another–food or yikes–into their instinct circuits. They have important matters to attend to, and they don't care whether I watch or not. And so I watch."

–Dave Barry

SNORKELING SITES

WHERE ARE THOSE BIG BEAUTIFUL FISH?

Maui is justifiably famous as a swimming, sunning, and snorkeling destination. Most of the great recreational sites are located on the more protected and relatively dry western side of the island.

For convenient snorkeling, the best areas to stay are West Maui (the Lahaina-Ka'anapali region), Kihei (very central), or the Wailea area (in the southwest). It really isn't a large island, so most sites (apart from the Hana area) are only a short drive if you stay anywhere along the west coast. Other sites are available by boat excursion from Lahaina or Ma'alaea Harbors.

West Maui offers numerous small, pretty bays. Some have large hotels or condos, others have no facilities at all. Large waves in the winter make snorkeling impossible at some bays in the northern end of West Maui, but other nearby bays shielded from swell can be surprisingly calm on the same day.

Kihei, located on flat land where the two mountains have formed a connection, is the most central place to stay, with convenient access to the highways as well as lower-priced condos and long stretches of sand. While you can see some fish here, there is much better snorkeling not that far away. Kihei's location makes a drive to the north or south quite easy. It doesn't quite have the charm or beauty of some other areas, but is still a good base for exploring the island.

The Wailea area, south of Kihei, has been growing, as huge new hotels have sprung up like wildflowers (or weeds, depending on whether you're staying there, or having to walk through them to get to your favorite beach). Like West Maui, it offers small, undeveloped bays as well as large beaches surrounded by hotels with all amenities. The bays aren't quite as calm as some in the north, but they can be excellent when conditions are good. It can be a bit drier than the north and has some outstandingly beautiful spots.

The entire west coast has plenty of hotels, condos, restaurants, shopping, excursions, hiking, golf, and nightlife. The far north and the far south also are very close to some charming, nearly deserted spots. The tall mountains tend to catch most of the rain, so you will usually (but not always) have plenty of sun in these leeward areas. The long stretches of sand are wonderful for lounging, but in Hawai'i, sand is a mixed blessing for snorkelers. Whenever swell rolls in, the sand and sediment gets churned up, making the water a

40

bit murky – especially after heavy rains, when muddy runoff flows. Don't expect 100' visibility, as some brochures imply, along the coast. There's still plenty to see, even with 30-60' visibility. Day trips to Molokini Island and Lana'i can take you to clearer waters when you're in the mood.

Maui has small, calm bays with white sandy beaches that are perfect for beginners. Coral, colorful fish, eels, turtles, and more are in easy reach – exciting for beginners and experienced snorkelers alike. More advanced snorkelers can cross the surf line and try the point at Mokule'ia for exceptionally colorful fish, or snorkel completely around a number of interesting points like Ulua-Mokapu, Makena Landing or Pu'u 'Ola'i.

There are countless excursions available to Molokini Island, and Lana'i is just a short boat ride from Lahaina. The channel between these islands is shallow making for a smooth trip most days. Consider taking either the ferry or an excursion to the friendly, uncrowded island of Lana'i, where the snorkeling is excellent.

In the section ahead, you'll find snorkeling site reviews organized from north to south, with more details about our favorites as well as those with special appeal, such as good beginner beaches. You'll also find details on Molokini Island, as well as the Island of Lana'i.

Many are surprisingly difficult to find, so bring these maps with you. People often drive up and down the highways with no idea which spots to try for snorkeling. Signs are scarce, so we've included clues and landmarks to help you find your spot.

Whatever your level of swimming or snorkeling ability, you can find a great spot to enjoy yourself along the west coast of Maui. When conditions are right, there are a few other sites farther afield that are worth a try. It's not possible to snorkel all the excellent sites in a week, so we hope that *Snorkel Hawai'i* will help you select a satisfying sample of the diverse snorkeling opportunities available on Maui and Lana'i.

TRUMPETFISH

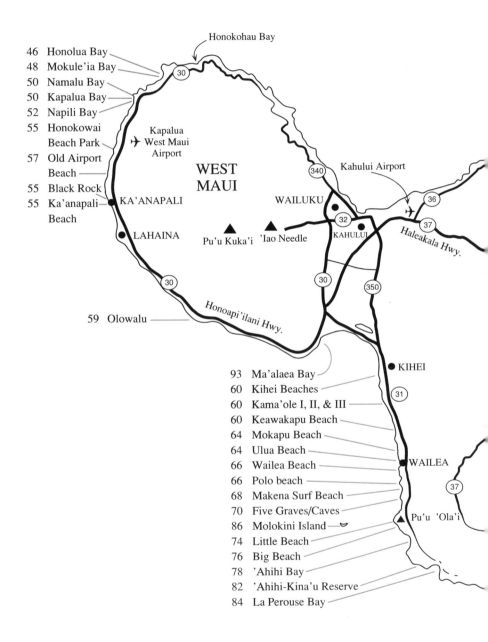

Honokohau Bay

46 Honolua Bay
48 Mokule'ia Bay
50 Namalu Bay
50 Kapalua Bay
52 Napili Bay
55 Honokowai
    Beach Park
57 Old Airport
    Beach
55 Black Rock
55 Ka'anapali
    Beach

Kapalua
West Maui
Airport

WEST
MAUI

Kahului Airport

WAILUKU

340

KA'ANAPALI

LAHAINA   Pu'u Kuka'i   'Iao Needle

32

KAHULUI   36

37

Haleakala Hwy.

30

30   350

59 Olowalu

Honoapi'ilani Hwy.

KIHEI

31

93 Ma'alaea Bay
60 Kihei Beaches
60 Kama'ole I, II, & III
60 Keawakapu Beach
64 Mokapu Beach
64 Ulua Beach
66 Wailea Beach
66 Polo beach
68 Makena Surf Beach
70 Five Graves/Caves
86 Molokini Island
74 Little Beach
76 Big Beach
78 'Ahihi Bay
82 'Ahihi-Kina'u Reserve
84 La Perouse Bay

WAILEA

37

Pu'u 'Ola'i

(Also see Road Map on page 4)

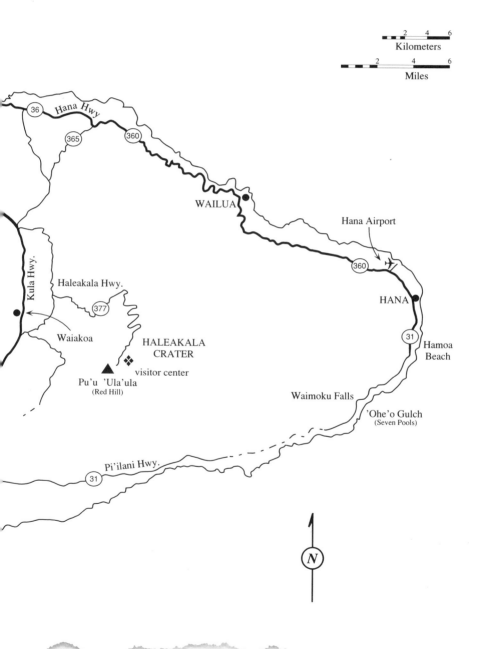

Kilometers

Miles

36 Hana Hwy

365

360

WAILUA

Hana Airport

360

Kula Hwy.

Haleakala Hwy.

HANA

377

31

Waiakoa

HALEAKALA
CRATER

Hamoa
Beach

visitor center

Pu'u 'Ula'ula
(Red Hill)

Waimoku Falls

'Ohe'o Gulch
(Seven Pools)

Pi'ilani Hwy.

31

N

SNORKELING SITES AT A GLANCE

	SNORKELING	ENTRY	SANDY BEACH	RESTROOM	SHOWERS	PICNIC AREA	SCENIC
Honolua Bay	A	1				•	•
Mokule'ia Bay	A	2-3	•			•	•
Namalu Bay	B	2					•
Kapalua Bay	A	1	•	•	•	•	•
Napili Bay	A	1	•	•	•	•	•
Honokowai	C	2-3	•	•	•	•	•
Ka'anapali	B	1	•	•	•	•	•
Kahekili	B	1	•	•	•	•	•
Olowalu	A	1	•			•	•
Keawakapu	C	1	•		•	•	•
Mokapu Beach	A	1	•	•	•	•	•
Ulua Beach	A	1	•	•	•	•	•
Wailea Beach	A	1	•	•	•	•	•
Chang's Beach	A	1	•				
Five Graves/Five Caves	A	3					•
Makena Landing	A	1	•	•	•	•	•
Maluaka Beach	A	1	•	•	•	•	•
Pu'u 'Ola'i	A	1	•				
Big Beach	C	1	•	•		•	•
'Ahihi Bay	A	1-2					•
'Ahihi-Kina'u	A	1-2				•	•
La Perouse Bay	A	3	•			•	•
Molokini Island	A	1					•
Manele Bay	A	2		•	•	•	•
Hulopo'e Bay	A	1	•	•	•	•	•
Pu'u Pehe Cove	A	2	•				•
Kaumalapa'u	A	2					
Club Lana'i	A	1	•	•	•	•	•

SHADE	PAGE	MAP PAGE	NOTES
•	46	47	fascinating, tops when calm
•	48	47	hike to lovely bay, excellent if calm
	50	51	slippery entrance, small
•	50	51	easy, pretty, usually very calm
•	52	51	large, calm bay between condos
•	55	42	very shallow, outer reef only
	55	54	long sand beach, often crowded
•	57	56	easy, pretty, nice beach
•	59	58	spacious, almost always calm, great coral
•	60	63	nice picnic spot
•	64	65	popular, near large hotels
•	64	65	very popular, all amenities, excellent
•	66	65	snorkel around point, turtles
•	68	69	small, well-hidden, delightful
•	70	71	excellent when clear, turtles, coves
•	70	71	tiny beach, long snorkel, very good
•	72	71	gorgeous, easy, excellent, don't miss
•	74	75	body surfing, hike to nude beach, excellent
•	76	75	sandy, good swim & picnic, near Pu'u 'Ola'i
•	78	79	small but fun, shallow, rocky
•	82	79	very secluded, hike over lava
•	84	79	great only if calm and clear
	86	87	very clear water, popular and crowded
•	114	115	tiny, varied fish, near harbor
•	114	115	big site, easy, outstanding and beautiful
•	117	115	requires hike and climb, excellent
	118	119	some uncommon fish, near barge harbor
•	94	109	from boat only, room to explore

HONOLUA BAY

Honolua Bay is the northern half of Honolua-Mokule'ia Bay Marine Life Conservation District. Both bays have the same sign, which can be confusing. Honolua Bay is a large bay that is usually quite well-protected, unless winter swells are rolling straight in. The bay can be murky after rain, as the muddy creek water flows in, but snorkeling can be very good, even with limited visibility.

If you park on the highway, as most folks do, you are treated to a short stroll down a dirt road through a beautiful canopied forest that feels almost like a jungle. If it has been raining, you will need to ford a small stream, usually not more than a foot deep.

When calm, Honolua Bay is heavenly and has something for everyone, beginner to advanced. You may enter anywhere along the rocky shore, but the easiest spot is in the center, where the road ends. There are remnants of an old concrete boat ramp. It's a bit slippery, but you can sit and work your way in slowly.

Snorkeling is best on the right side as far as the point, but the center has dramatic deep canyons. We've seen many exceptionally large fish and turtles there. The left is good, too, so snorkel all over the bay if time allows and conditions are good. If it's a calm day, snorkel around the point at the left into the next bay, but not as far in as the surf line. Be sure to check out all the little coves along the way.

You'll see large, colorful fish: huge tangs, parrot fish, butterfly fish of all kinds, ornate wrasses, scrawled filefish, rectangular triggerfish, lei triggerfish, eels, huge turtles, and healthy coral in orange, pink, and light blue. This is a beautiful spot for a picnic under deep shade in a jungle setting. The small semi-sandy beach is a bit rocky for swimming. Don't miss this one! You'll want to return.

GETTING THERE   *Head north on Highway 30 past Ka'anapali and Kapalua (see map, page 47). At .6 mile past marker 32 you'll see a dirt road down to the bay. You can park along the road on the beach side. With 4-wheel drive, you can usually make it down this short bare dirt road (and park in the shade!), but don't cross the stream bed near the end if it looks like rain. There is space for a few cars off the side of the road just before the stream and more at the beach itself. Walking down is easy and beautiful through this miniature rain forest. Rains can quickly cause the river to rise, so be prepared to wade through if necessary. Reef shoes are handy for this and can save you from injury. There are no facilities here.*

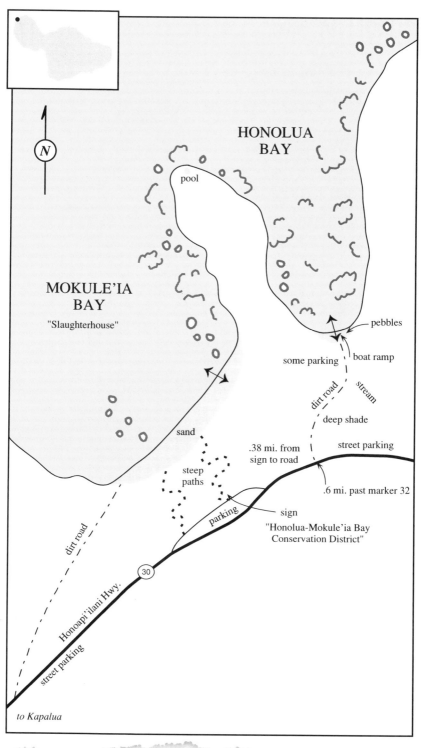

HONOLUA
BAY

N

MOKULE'IA
BAY

"Slaughterhouse"

pool

pebbles

some parking

boat ramp

stream

dirt road

deep shade

sand

.38 mi. from
sign to road

street parking

steep
paths

.6 mi. past marker 32

parking

sign

"Honolua-Mokule'ia Bay
Conservation District"

dirt road

30

Honoapi'ilani Hwy.

street parking

street parking

to Kapalua

MOKULE'IA BAY

Often referred to by its nickname "Slaughterhouse", this bay is just south of Honolua Bay, and is easily confused with it, since the signs are identical. If you see a steep path leading down a high bluff, rather than a fairly flat dirt road, you're at Mokule'ia. Two paths lead down the hillside, and a major improvement is in the works for one path. Until that happens, you need adequate footwear to hike in on the steep trails.

This site tends to have rougher surf, but has a nice sandy beach, good swimming, picnicking and terrific snorkeling just beyond the surf on the right. We saw a very colorful assortment of fish here: yellowtail coris, pinktail triggerfish, Christmas wrasse, lei triggerfish, orangespine unicornfish, orangeband surgeonfish, and much more. Since this beach requires a longer hike and often requires better swimming skills, head for Honolua Bay, the very next bay to the north, if you're a beginner.

Mokule'ia is a wonderful place with little coves to explore and has some of the more colorful fish anywhere on Maui. Pink and orange seem to be popular fish colors at this site for some odd reason. The point to the right is easy to swim around if conditions are calm, so it's hard to resist snorkeling on over to Honolua Bay – or at least to some of the interesting little coves along the way. These two bays are not for any snorkeler when the surf gets heavy. Big swell rolls in most of the time in the winter, and it gets rough any time of year if swell rolls straight in. These bays then become fine surfing sites.

Warning: Unless you are well-experienced, snorkel here only in the mornings when quite calm, since waves can pick up unexpectedly.

GETTING THERE   *Go north on Highway 30 to .1 mile past marker 32* (see map, page 47). *Or from Honolua, go .3 mile south on Highway 30. You'll see cars parked on the beach side of the highway in two locations. Both spots are the start of steep trails down to the beach. The south trail is easier, while the one to the north is closer to the good snorkeling. This trail starts at the sign: "Honolua-Mokule'ia Bay Marine Life Conservation District". There are several identical signs, so look for telephone pole 281 X. The trail heads down just to the left of the sign. You need to have good balance and wear appropriate shoes for either of these trails, but it's not far. If the trails are blocked, walk back south (toward Kapalua) to find the dirt road. Remember that no facilities are available at this beach.*

Doctor my eyes

If you are swimming along snorkeling peacefully, and your vision suddenly gets totally out of focus, don't be too quick to panic and call for a doctor. While you may have had a stroke, there is a much more likely cause:

You've probably just entered into an outdoor demonstration of the refractive qualities of mixtures of clear liquids of different densities. Is that perfectly clear?

Near the edge of some protected bays, clear spring water oozes smoothly out into the saltwater. As it is lighter than the mineral-laden saltwater, it tends to float in a layer near the surface for a time.

Now, clear spring water is easy to see through, as is clear saltwater. If you mix them thoroughly, you have dilute saltwater, still clear. But when the two float side by side, the light going through them is bent and re-bent as it passes between them, and this blurs your vision. It's much like the blurring produced when hot, lighter air rises off black pavement, and produces wavy vision and mirage.

These lenses of clear water drift about, and often disappear as quickly as they appeared. Swimming away from the source of the spring water usually solves the problem. Clear at last?

CHRISTMAS WRASSE

NAMALU BAY

Just north of Kapalua Bay and directly in front of the Kapalua Bay Resort, you'll find a small, pretty bay lined with rocks. It has good snorkeling, although not quite as good as Kapalua. The rocky entry is quite slippery and the water a bit less calm. If you're curious and conditions are calm, it's quite easy to snorkel around the point to the left and end up on Kapalua Beach.

GETTING THERE   *Park in the public parking area for Kapalua Bay (access #219), walk down the steps to the right and continue on the path to the far side of the broad beach. From the end of the beach it's just a short walk of about 100 yards through the hotel grounds to cross the point* (see map, page 51).

KAPALUA BAY

This popular postcard-perfect beach just south of the Kapalua Bay Resort has terrific snorkeling and easy entry anywhere along its lovely crescent of sand.

The best snorkeling is on the right as far as the point, although the whole bay is interesting: left, center and even close to shore. When the surf kicks up along the west coast, try heading here, because it's usually as calm as Maui gets. Public parking is limited to about 25 cars and the lot fills early. There is no alternative parking available anywhere close, unless you want to park anyway and risk a ticket.

Afternoons are pleasant, because this bay tends to stay calm and the crowds diminish. Showers and restrooms are available on the beach side of the public parking lot. Once you find a parking space, the path to the beach is short with some steps along the way.

The bay is small, so you can swim around the whole area if you wish. We saw eels, a turtle, an octopus, as well as most of the usual colorful fish that call Maui home. A good swimmer can easily snorkel around the point to the left and end up at Napili Bay – only a short hike back to your car if you cut directly through the condo developments. If you decide to try this, the best place to exit is the sandy corner near the shower *(see map, page 51)*.

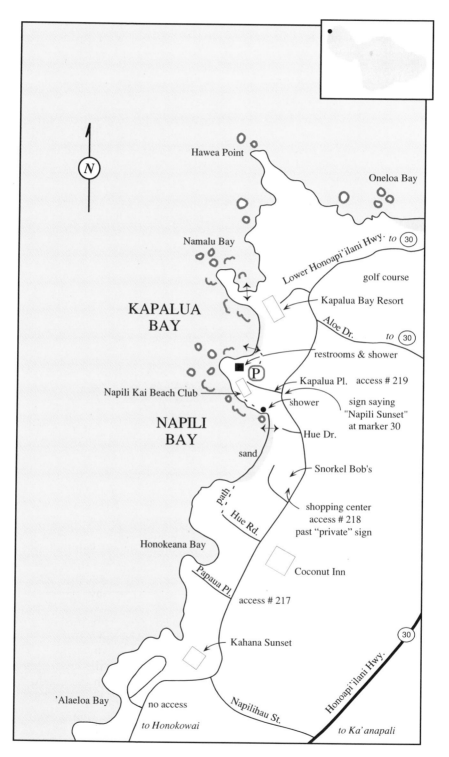

Hawea Point

Oneloa Bay

Namalu Bay

Lower Honoapi'ilani Hwy. *to* 30

golf course

KAPALUA
BAY

Kapalua Bay Resort

Aloe Dr. *to* 30

restrooms & shower

P

Kapalua Pl.   access # 219

Napili Kai Beach Club

shower

sign saying
"Napili Sunset"
at marker 30

NAPILI
BAY

Hue Dr.

sand

Snorkel Bob's

path

shopping center
access # 218
past "private" sign

Hue Rd.

Honokeana Bay

Coconut Inn

Papaua Pl.

access # 217

30

Kahana Sunset

'Alaeloa Bay

no access

to Honokowai

Napilihau St.

Honoapi'ilani Hwy.

to Ka'anapali

51

GETTING THERE   *Kapalua Bay has just one public access, #219 (see map, page 51). Look sharp, as it's easy to miss the sign. Parking fills up early, but often has plenty of space later in the day. Drive north on Highway 30, past Ka'anapali and take the next major Y to the left, which is Lower Honoapi'ilani Road, following the coast. Just .1 mile north of marker 30, you'll see the Napili Kai Beach Club on your left and a little blue beach access sign on the right. Turn left here and park in the public lot at the end of the road on the right. You'll see the showers and restrooms toward the beach. The path heads down the steps to the right of the restrooms.*

PINKTAIL TRIGGERFISH

NAPILI BAY

Much larger than Kapalua Bay, this next bay to the south offers similar snorkeling on the right side. It's a beautiful place to picnic, swim, sun or snorkel. Napili Bay is completely surrounded by condos, so there are often plenty of people here sharing the sandy beach. If you want to snorkel, try to park at the far north because it's a long walk across the beach otherwise.

Entry is easy from the sand, but you can also enter from the rocks in several places from the path in front of the condos along the right point. Although Napili Bay has three public access signs, there is very little parking available, so come early, or later in the afternoon. We enjoyed the very clear water here, and saw wrasses, triggerfish, all kinds of butterflyfish, eels, Moorish idols, a school of trumpetfish, needlefish, and parrotfish. A shower is available, but restrooms are located at the Kapalua parking lot.

GETTING THERE *Napili has three public beach access signs, but all are easy to miss, and none offers much parking (see map, page 51). Going north on Highway 30 past Ka'anapali, take the next major Y to the left, Lower Honoapi'ilani Road, and follow this road north along the coast, past 'Alaeloa.*

When you see signs for the various Napili condos, watch for little blue beach access signs. Each offers a bit of on-street parking. Access point #219 is the furthest north, so using it gets you closer to the best snorkeling. Walk to the left instead of the right (Kapalua is to the right). Just steps from the best entry, there is also a small shower tucked away at the corner of the beach along the walkway in front of the condos. Access point #218 is cleverly hidden behind the shopping center. Just continue driving toward the water past Snorkel Bob's (ignoring the warning sign) and there it is! There are also a few parking spaces on Hue Drive. All of the Napili parking is on the street, except for the Kapalua lot.

'ALAELOA

'Alaeloa has a small beach called The Cove. This charming little beach, without much sand, looks like it could have good snorkeling with space to explore from a pebbled entry. Getting to the beach is the main problem, as the only land access is private property. The surrounding development has a gate and the houses are rented on a monthly basis, so it isn't easy to gain entrance. This development went in before public access was a big issue, and they seem quite determined to keep it private.

GETTING THERE *Finding 'Alaeloa is easy (see map, page 51). There's only one way in and it has a prominent sign on Lower Honoapi'ilani Road. The gate is the only entrance. It would be a long swim from any other bay. A boat could drop you off and pick you up later, or you might kayak in.*

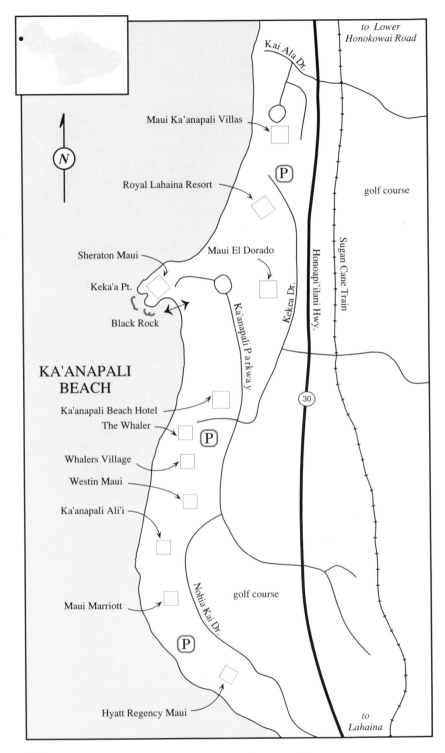

to Lower
Honokowai Road

Kai Ala Dr.

Maui Ka'anapali Villas

golf course

Royal Lahaina Resort

Sheraton Maui

Maui El Dorado

Keka'a Pt.

Black Rock

KA'ANAPALI
BEACH

Ka'anapali Beach Hotel

The Whaler

Whalers Village

Westin Maui

Ka'anapali Ali'i

Maui Marriott

golf course

Hyatt Regency Maui

to
Lahaina

Ka'anapali Parkway

Kekea Dr.

Honoapi'ilani Hwy.

Sugan Cane Train

Nohia Kai Dr.

30

N

54

HONOKOWAI BEACH PARK

The reef here is very shallow, making swimming difficult and a bit hazardous at times. At low tide, however, there are tide pools perfect for little children. To get beyond the shallow part, swim out at the far north of the park (to your right). Only the ocean side of the reef is deep enough for snorkeling, so go on a very calm day and try for a high tide. This is not a good place for beginners. You'll find a shady, grassy park with picnic tables, facilities, and a store right across the street in case you forgot to bring a picnic.

GETTING THERE   *This park is easy to spot along Lower Honoapi'ilani Road and has plenty of parking. Going north from Ka'anapali on Hwy. 30, angle left on Lower Honoapi'ilani Road and watch for the first beach on your left. You'll find it across the street from a market and the Aston Maui Park Hotel. On the ocean side you will see a square grassy area with picnic tables, restrooms and shower.*

KA'ANAPALI BEACH

One of Maui's big, beautiful beaches that has suffered from overdevelopment, becoming home to numerous huge hotels. Snorkel the far right of Ka'anapali Beach to the point, Black Rock, or even beyond to a little cove if it's calm. This is a very long beach, so park as far north as you can. There are some large and very tame fish. Beware of people jumping off the cliff – it's a very popular sport here. Don't expect lots of coral or particularly clear water. This site seems to be somewhat overused and overrated. Still, it's worth a swim if you're in the vicinity.

GETTING THERE   *Ka'anapali is easy to find going north on Highway 30 past Lahaina* (see map, page 54). *Parking is a problem. To snorkel you need to park as far north as possible, because this beach is much too long to walk (although it does have a long promenade). From Highway 30, follow the signs to the big hotels and take Ka'anapali Parkway to either side of the Sheraton Maui. Black Rock is directly in front of the hotel. There are beach access lanes between some of these large hotels where you may drop off passengers, but the only parking is in the hotel lots.*

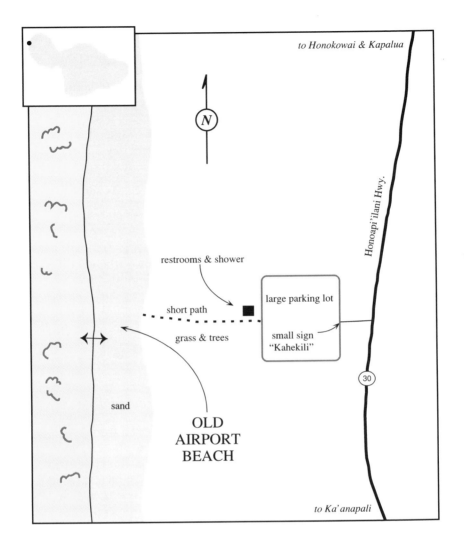

to Honokowai & Kapalua

N

Honoapi'ilani Hwy.

restrooms & shower

short path

large parking lot

grass & trees

small sign
"Kahekili"

30

sand

OLD
AIRPORT
BEACH

to Ka'anapali

56

KAHEKILI

Kahekili is usually called **Old Airport Beach**, since it is located near the former site of the West Maui airport. This is an enjoyable snorkeling, swimming, and picnicking beach north of Ka'anapali. It's easy to drive right by Kahekili, because the beach is somewhat hidden from the highway.

Watch for a large parking lot near the highway. This park has plenty of grass, restrooms, and showers. You have to park and walk about one minute to see the beach, which is very pretty, with plenty of shade trees. Snorkel directly in front, but don't stray out too far if it's at all rough. A very popular snorkeling site, it has easy entry from the sand and immediate snorkeling well protected by the outer reef. When calm, this park is a good place for beginning snorkelers.

GETTING THERE   *Kahekili can be reached from Highway 30 just north of Ka'anapali. Watch for a park on the beach side and the Sugar Cane Train on the left* (see map, page 56). *You won't see the sand from the highway, but you will see a large parking lot. A little sign in the parking lot says "Kahekili." After parking, walk toward the water, passing the restrooms and picnic area till you see the sand.*

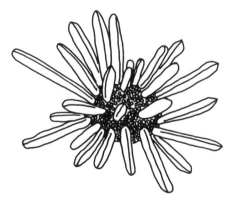

SLATEPENCIL SEA URCHIN

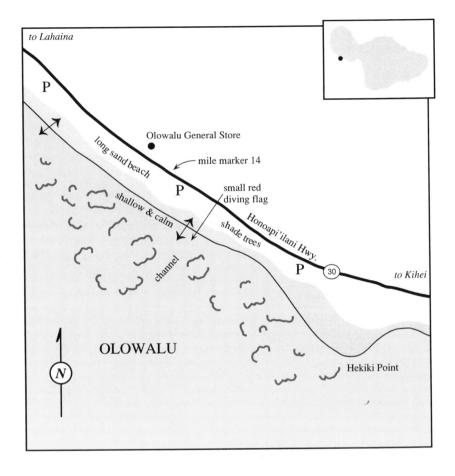

to Lahaina

P

Olowalu General Store

long sand beach

mile marker 14

P

small red
diving flag

shallow & calm

Honoapi'ilani Hwy.

shade trees

channel

P 30

to Kihei

N

OLOWALU

Hekiki Point

PICASSO TRIGGERFISH

OLOWALU

Olowalu Beach is a very long beach with good snorkeling almost anywhere. The most famous spot is called "Mile 14", since it's near that highway marker. This large, almost always calm, easy snorkeling area has something for everyone. Its long stretch of soft sandy beach has plenty of shade trees and easy entry points. Beginners and children can stay very near shore.

Better snorkelers can weave around the extensive reefs for a great distance out to sea, left or right. The coral here is very large and mostly quite healthy. There's plenty to see in every direction and it could hardly be easier as long as it's calm – which is quite common because the reef extends so far out to sea and offers protection from the surf. At this site, parking is no problem at all. You'll see cars parked along the highway the whole length of the beach.

There is a diver's flag marking the main channel out through the reef. You don't need to limit yourself to snorkeling by the flag, unless you're particularly concerned about having a twenty-foot wide channel to head out through the coral. There are several other passages through the reef. When calm, even a beginner would have no problem finding an easy passage. No facilities are located here. Drive south to find restrooms, a few portables along the road.

GETTING THERE   *Just south of marker 14 on Highway 30, just south of the Olowalu General Store, is an extensive area for swimming and snorkeling* (see map, page 58). *There's plenty of parking on the ocean side of the highway, with some shade available. You'll see clusters of cars at popular spots. You might want to try the center first, then return another day to explore this exceptionally broad reef area.*

RECTANGULAR TRIGGERFISH

KIHEI AREA

The Kihei area offers plenty of condos and plenty of sand (*see map, page 61*). While this isn't the best area to snorkel, the beach is about six miles long, so there's ample room to swim and sun. The beaches called Kama'ole I, II, and III (usually called Kam I, II, and III) can be seen as you travel south on Kihei Road. They each have public facilities including parking, restrooms, and showers.

The town itself has markets, shopping, banks, and restaurants. This can be a cooler part of Maui in the summer because the winds often blow across this low area between Maui's high mountains. There is a wide range of condos to choose from (some very inexpensive) and the area is quite central for excursions around the island, so it's not a bad location for snorkelers as long as you don't expect to snorkel right there all the time. We prefer to be located a bit outside the town to avoid the crowds. The long stretches of sand and fairly calm water make this a popular spot for families with young children. While the center of town is somewhat crowded, the condos at each end of town (especially toward Ma'alaea) are often very quiet.

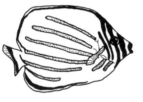

ORNATE BUTTERFLYFISH

KEAWAKAPU BEACH PARK

This beach, located between Kihei and Wailea, is charming and calm, though not terrific for snorkeling. It's a great place to swim, picnic and enjoy the view. There is a shower, but no restrooms.

GETTING THERE   *Take Highway 31 south from Kihei, turning right at Kilohana Drive. You'll come to South Kihei Road, where you'll find beach access #108. Or you can also drive south through the town of Kihei on South Kihei Road. The parking lot has about 25 spaces* (see map, page 63).

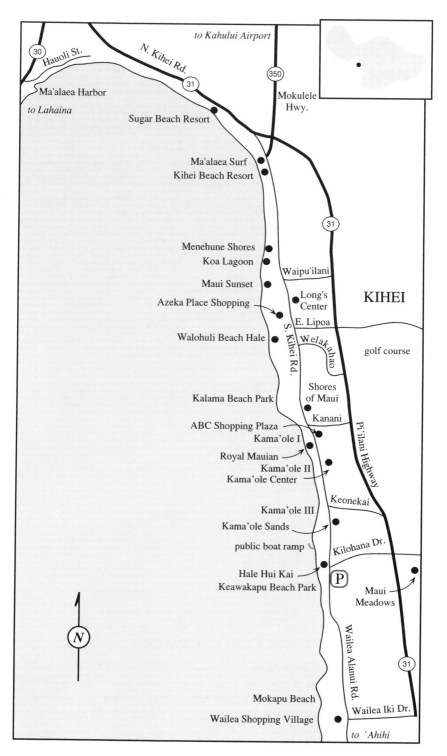

to Kahului Airport

30 Hauoli St.
N. Kihei Rd.
31
350
Ma'alaea Harbor
to Lahaina
Mokulele
Hwy.
Sugar Beach Resort

Ma'alaea Surf
Kihei Beach Resort

31

Menehune Shores
Koa Lagoon
Waipu'ilani
Maui Sunset
Azeka Place Shopping
Long's
Center
E. Lipoa
Walohuli Beach Hale
Welakahao

KIHEI

golf course

S. Kihei Rd.

Shores
of Maui
Kalama Beach Park
Kanani
ABC Shopping Plaza
Kama'ole I
Royal Mauian
Kama'ole II
Kama'ole Center
Keonekai
Kama'ole III
Kama'ole Sands
public boat ramp
Kilohana Dr.
Hale Hui Kai
Keawakapu Beach Park
P
Maui
Meadows

Pi'ilani Highway

N

Wailea Alanui Rd.

31

Mokapu Beach
Wailea Shopping Village
Wailea Iki Dr.
to 'Ahihi

61

WAILEA AREA

The western side of East Maui has been growing rapidly in recent years. This is a beautiful area located beneath the rain shadow of Haleakala with views of several islands off the coast. Several huge hotels of various styles have been built on terrific beaches. Other equally nice beaches remain secluded as ever.

There are relatively few condos here (but some are excellent) and prices are usually high. Hotel styles and sizes really vary, so select a hotel to your taste or choose a good beach and settle for what accommodations are there. This is really a great place for snorkelers, from beginners to advanced. It's not quite as calm as the little bays in West Maui, but it has plenty of coves, points, beaches, and some lava fields.

The variety reaches out to sea and attracts lots of turtles and interesting fish. All in all, an excellent location for serious snorkelers. If the prices seem too steep for your pocketbook, stay in the Kihei area and drive here to snorkel. Kihei has an abundance of condos of every price and quality. Many of the nicest ones are located a bit away from the crowded town, so require a car anyway.

Wailea is becoming more and more popular, so it's easy to see that development will continue toward the south. Highway 31 will gradually be extended as the land is developed.

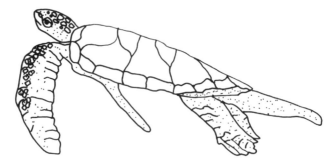

GREEN SEATURTLE

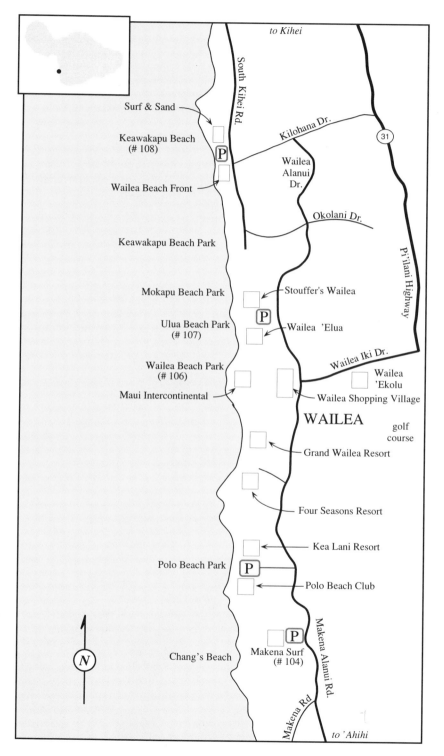

to Kihei

South Kihei Rd.

Surf & Sand

Keawakapu Beach
(# 108)

P

Wailea Beach Front

Kilohana Dr.

31

Wailea
Alanui
Dr.

Okolani Dr.

Keawakapu Beach Park

Mokapu Beach Park

Stouffer's Wailea

P

Ulua Beach Park
(# 107)

Wailea 'Elua

Wailea Iki Dr.

Pi'ilani Highway

Wailea Beach Park
(# 106)

Maui Intercontinental

Wailea
'Ekolu

Wailea Shopping Village

WAILEA

golf
course

Grand Wailea Resort

Four Seasons Resort

Kea Lani Resort

Polo Beach Park

P

Polo Beach Club

N

Chang's Beach

P

Makena Surf
(# 104)

Makena Alanui Rd.

Makena Rd

to 'Ahihi

63

ULUA BEACH PARK

At this very popular snorkeling and shore diving spot, you can snorkel on around the point to the right, or far out to sea as well. Coral and fish are plentiful. Picnic on the grassy hill and enjoy the view. All amenities are right here.

This is a very popular spot, so come early or late if you want to avoid crowds. Experienced snorkelers can simply swim beyond most snorkelers, who tend to stay close to shore. This is an excellent site, with lots to see, a beautiful setting, and a reasonable amount of parking.

GETTING THERE   *Ulua is the beach in front of the Stouffer Wailea Beach Resort, with lots of big resorts nearby* (see map, page 65). *Take Highway 31 south past Kihei and watch for Wailea-Iki Drive to the right heading toward the resorts. At the Wailea Shopping Village turn right on Wailea Alanui Road toward the Stouffer Wailea Beach Resort. You'll quickly see a large sign for Mokapu-Ulua Beach. This is public access #107. Drop people and gear at the beach near the showers and restrooms, then send the driver off to locate a parking spot.*

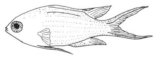

BLUE CHROMIS

MOKAPU BEACH

Mokapu Beach is where you end up if you snorkel completely around the point from Ulua Beach. Just to be different, you can begin your snorkel here and end up at Ulua – assuming you plan to snorkel the whole point. It would be too far for most beginners, but is quite easy for an intermediate snorkeler. This makes an excellent one-way snorkel if you have a way to handle the transportation back to your car. Mornings tend to be a bit calmer here. Further north is Mokapu Beach Park.

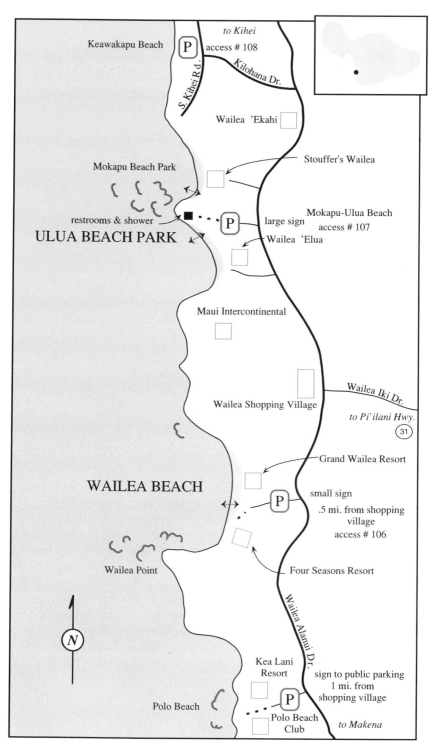

Keawakapu Beach

P

to Kihei
access # 108

Kilohana Dr.

S. Kihei Rd.

Wailea 'Ekahi

Stouffer's Wailea

Mokapu Beach Park

restrooms & shower

ULUA BEACH PARK

P

large sign

Mokapu-Ulua Beach
access # 107

Wailea 'Elua

Maui Intercontinental

Wailea Shopping Village

Wailea Iki Dr.

to Pi'ilani Hwy.
(31)

Grand Wailea Resort

WAILEA BEACH

P

small sign

.5 mi. from shopping
village
access # 106

Wailea Point

Four Seasons Resort

Wailea Alanui Dr.

N

Kea Lani
Resort

P

sign to public parking
1 mi. from
shopping village

Polo Beach

Polo Beach
Club

to Makena

WAILEA BEACH

The next beach south of Ulua is Wailea, which has excellent
snorkeling as well. A rocky point provides similar habitat, so you
can snorkel out around it to see turtles, eels and plenty of fish.
Depending on the day, you might even see more here, although Ulua
has the better reputation. You might even prefer this site since it's
not quite so crowded, but come early to park. All these exposed sites
can have waves that pick up in the afternoon, so come early for
parking, quiet and great snorkeling. This is another nice spot to
linger for a picnic. Because of the nearby hotels, all amenities are
available here.

GETTING THERE   *This beach is between the Grand Hyatt Wailea
Resort to the south, and the Four Seasons Hotel to the north
(see map, page 65). From Highway 31, turn right on Wailea-Iki Drive,
then left on Wailea Alanui Road at the Wailea Shopping Village to the
first public access (access # 106), which has 24 parking spaces. Take
the path directly to the beach. You'll see the shower and restroom on
the right of the path. When you reach the sand, snorkel to the left
towards the point and around if calm enough.*

POLO BEACH

Not the best snorkeling or swimming around, but it's OK and there
is public access, adequate parking and good facilities. It's also a
charming spot to picnic. Polo Beach is located between the huge
white Kea Lani Hotel (which can't be missed, even if you close your
eyes) and the tall Polo Beach condos. The beach is a little rocky, but
it's very picturesque.

GETTING THERE   *From Highway 31, take a right toward Wailea, then a
left on Wailea Alanui Road when you must turn (see map, page 65).
From this corner, continue 1 mile south on Wailea Alanui Road to the
public access for Polo Beach parking. It's a nice park with a path to the
beach, restrooms, shower, picnic tables and a lovely view.*

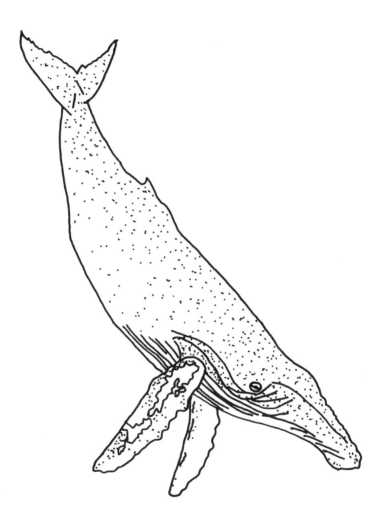

HUMPBACK WHALE

MAKENA SURF

Chang's Beach (better known as Makena Surf) is an easily-missed, but delightful beach with excellent swimming and snorkeling. The beach is entirely surrounded by the two-story Makena Surf condos, but good public access is provided, if you look carefully. No public facilities are available, though.

This beach is really a small, perfect gem in every way, and is one of our Maui favorites. It combines a pretty and serene beach, hard to beat easy access from sand for swimming, sailing or kayaking, usually calm water, and wonderful snorkeling.

As usual in Maui on an exposed beach, waves can pick up in the afternoon, so come early. The large, deluxe condos are available for rent, and make a great family location if the rental rates don't send you into shock.

GETTING THERE   *Go south on Highway 31, turning right toward Wailea on Wailea Iki Drive, then left on Wailea Alanui Road when you come to the big shopping center and have to turn one way or the other (see map, page 61). Turn left and continue south for 3.5 miles from this intersection. Watch for the rock walls surrounding the Makena Surf. There is a small entrance to a 9-car public parking lot with a little blue "public access #104" sign posted in an inconspicuous spot.*

The paved, shady trail starts at the front left of the parking lot where you will go through a green gate (see map, page 69). Just follow the trail downhill through the flowers to the beach. Then snorkel the left side of the beach, which is just steps from the end of the trail.

Finding your way back up to your car can be the hardest part. It's all too easy to wander off on one of the side trails that dead-end at sections of the condos. From the beach, the trail leads straight to a Y. Be sure to angle right here. The next Y leads to a shower on the right, but your car will be waiting in the parking lot that you reach by going left. Check our map. If you end up in the wrong parking lot, you won't even be able to get out to the street due to the gates, so you'll have to double back almost to the beach.

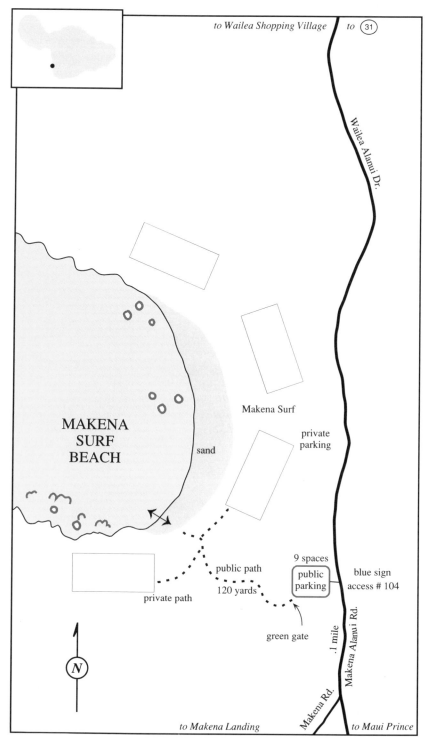

to Wailea Shopping Village   to ⟨31⟩

Wailea Alanui Dr.

MAKENA
SURF
BEACH

sand

Makena Surf

private
parking

public path

120 yards

private path

9 spaces

public
parking

blue sign
access # 104

green gate

.1 mile

Makena Alanui Rd.

N

Makena Rd.

to Makena Landing   to Maui Prince

FIVE GRAVES/CAVES

This popular area includes several entries ranging in difficulty from beginner to advanced and is often snorkeled by boat access. There are plenty of turtles in the area as well as interesting canyons and coves. It's often a better site for Scuba than snorkeling, when conditions are a little rougher. It has a tendency to be choppy as well as murky.

Still, on a nice day it can make for very enjoyable snorkeling, especially when the visibility is good enough to see the turtles. They often rest on the bottom which is 15 to 20' deep here. Look sharp in sandy pockets among the coral and you'll be rewarded.

GETTING THERE   *Go south on Highway 31, turning left toward Wailea on Wailea Iki Drive, then right at the Wailea Shopping Center on Wailea Alanui Road* (see map, page 61). *Watch for Makena Road to your right just past the Makena Surf condos. Just .2 mile from the turnoff, you'll reach the Five Graves area* (see map, page 71). *There is a tiny parking area on the beach side of the road (about 10 cars) and a short path heads towards the water, passing the graves. This path angles to the right toward a narrow cove where divers often enter. Entering from this cove is definitely not for beginners because the rocks are slippery and the surf unpredictable here. It does get you right in the middle of the best snorkeling though.*

For a much easier access, but longer swim, continue on Makena Road to the Makena Landing County Park (access # 103), where you'll find a parking lot on the right with a shower and restrooms on the left near the sand (see map, page 71).

MAKENA LANDING

Entry is best at the right side in the corner near the parking lot. There is a small, sandy beach offering easy access. Snorkel to the right and around the point as far as seems calm.

Another entry point (over rock) is from the middle of the parking lot. It's a bit trickier, but handy if the water's calm enough and you're careful to not slip on the rocks. This gets you out closer to the point where you'll find the best snorkeling. There is also a neat little entry cove just ten feet beyond the parking lot, but it's marked "private property". See GETTING THERE for Five Graves above.

70

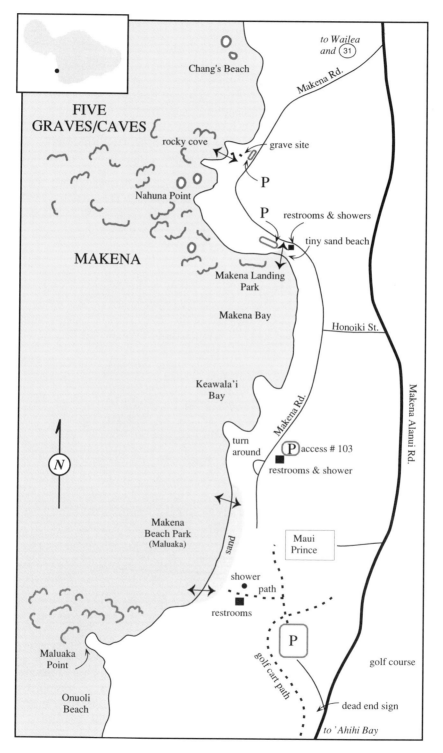

FIVE GRAVES/CAVES

Chang's Beach

to Wailea
and (31)

Makena Rd.

rocky cove

grave site

P

Nahuna Point

P

restrooms & showers

tiny sand beach

MAKENA

Makena Landing
Park

Makena Bay

Honoiki St.

Keawala'i
Bay

N

turn
around

Makena Rd.

P access # 103

restrooms & shower

Makena
Beach Park
(Maluaka)

Maui
Prince

Makena Alanui Rd.

sand

shower

path

restrooms

P

golf cart path

golf course

Maluaka
Point

dead end sign

Onuoli
Beach

to 'Ahihi Bay

71

MALUAKA BEACH

Makena Beach Park (Maluaka Beach in front of the Maui Prince Hotel) is an excellent all-around site. The south end of this lovely beach offers wonderful snorkeling and easy entry from the sand. It is serene, relatively uncrowded, and home to an unusually large number of turtles. We also saw some Picasso triggerfish right near shore. This elegant fish is also called "lagoon triggerfish".

At the far south end of the beach there is a grassy hill with gorgeous views, picnic tables, shade, restrooms and showers. This is a delightful swimming, snorkeling, or picnic spot. The view includes Molokini, Lana'i, Kaho'olawe, Pu'u 'Ola'i (the cinder cone beyond Big Beach), and West Maui in the distance.

Maluaka also tends to be fairly calm, so can be great for beginning snorkelers. The further out you swim, the more turtles you'll see. This is where we saw the largest one we've encountered. Mornings are best, since the swells can pick up in the afternoon. This is one of Maui's prettiest spots and remains surprisingly uncrowded.

GETTING THERE   *Going south on Highway 31, turn right toward Wailea on Wailea Iki Drive (see map, page 61). Highway 31 dead ends here at the moment, although it may eventually be extended. At the Wailea Shopping Center turn left on Wailea Alanui Road. Note your mileage at this point. In 3.6 miles you'll see a small road on your right that doubles back and has a sign that says "dead end". It's very easy to miss if you forget to note the mileage (see map, page 71). There is a golf path on the far side of the little road, so you'll know it's the right one. Take this a short few blocks to the small parking lot holding about 20 cars. There's a nice, easy path to the beach – about 100 yards. You'll see restrooms and picnic tables on your left. To the right is a shower. Snorkel along the reef on the left, which is quite extensive. In calm weather, you can snorkel directly over the reef with plenty of clearance. Stay beyond the edge when swells get higher.*

An alternative access to this beach is from Makena Road leading to the the north end of the beach. You'll find a public parking lot on the left side of the road with restrooms and shower about 200 yards before you get to the north end of the beach. Passengers can be dropped off much closer. From this end of the beach you can snorkel to the right or hike across the beach and snorkel the southern side.

Be a good guest

Remember that Maui residents pay substantial taxes to provide lifeguards, showers (even when water is scarce) and clean up after wild tropical weather. You are given entirely free access to these fragile environments, while crowding the streets with rental cars, and certainly not contributing to the serenity.

You can help balance this by buying local products and crafts whenever you can. It's not that hard to do, or especially expensive, and is good for Hawai'i.

Try to leave each beach a little better than when you arrived. If you can surface dive, use your skills to retrieve that soft drink can resting on the bottom. Anyone, even small children, can pick up a bit of trash on the beach. Take that glass bottle away so it won't get broken and cut your feet next time.

This is something special that you can give to the people who live here and the people who will visit in the future, perhaps even your own grandchildren. Help preserve the kind of environment you'd like to live in and hand over to your children: beautiful Hawai'i.

REEF SQUID

PU'U 'OLA'I BEACH

Pu'u 'Ola'i is also called **Little Beach**. From the parking lot at Oneloa, also called "Big Beach", where the sign says "Makena State Park", walk straight down the shady, flat path to the long, sandy beach with some facilities (picnic tables, portable toilets, no shower) and a lifeguard at times.

This is a very popular, sunny, swimming and sunbathing spot with some shade. Just beyond the lifeguard station at the far right is a path leading up the hill to Little Beach, which is a traditional nude beach. It also happens to be an excellent snorkeling spot when calm.

Snorkel to the right as far as it's calm enough. There are lots of little canyons, coves, good coral, large and numerous turtles, and plenty of fish variety (although not huge numbers of fish). The snorkeling is definitely worth the hike. When calm, you can snorkel all the way around the point to the next beach, with good snorkeling the entire way. An experienced and strong snorkeler can swim north to Makena Beach (the one in front of the Maui Prince Hotel), although it's a long walk back to the car from here.

Note: To avoid confusion, remember there are other Makena and Oneloa beaches on Maui, thus the popularity of the name "Big".

GETTING THERE   *Going south on Highway 31, turn right toward the Wailea Shopping Center, then left and continue south* (see map, page 61). *The Big Beach turnoff is 4 miles south of this point* (see map, page 75). *This is the old parking lot, but provides the best access to the north end of the beach, and to Little Beach. A new and larger one has been built just to the south. At the beach side of the parking lot is a path marked with a sign that says "Makena State Park". Follow it 180 yards to the beach, then continue across the sand to the right past the lifeguard station until you see the narrow path over the small hill (about 50' high) 240 yards to Little Beach. It's a fairly easy path, but not flat, and requires some minor climbing over the hill.*

BIRD WRASSE

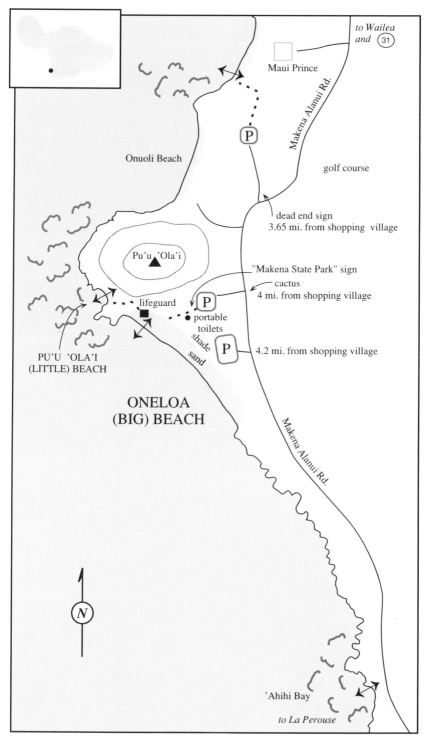

to Wailea
and (31)

Maui Prince

Makena Alanui Rd.

P

golf course

Onuoli Beach

dead end sign
3.65 mi. from shopping village

Pu'u 'Ola'i ▲

"Makena State Park" sign
cactus
4 mi. from shopping village

P

lifeguard ■

portable
toilets

P

4.2 mi. from shopping village

PU'U 'OLA'I
(LITTLE) BEACH

shade
sand

ONELOA
(BIG) BEACH

Makena Alanui Rd.

N

'Ahihi Bay
to La Perouse

75

ONELOA BEACH

This popular beach, usually referred to as **Big Beach**, is best for swimming, sunning, picnics and socializing. It often has a fair surf, and is popular for body surfing and boogie boarding. At times, it can be too rough for safety.

Snorkeling is best around the point between Big and Little Beaches, and is possible only when conditions are calm enough. It is possible to snorkel all the way to Little Beach from the northern end near the lifeguard station at Big Beach.

Most people would prefer to hike over to Little Beach rather than cross through breakers, but it is possible if you're a strong swimmer. If you want to snorkel, be sure to park in the lot at the far north since this is indeed one **BIG** Beach. You'll find plenty of wide sandy beach, picnic tables, portable toilets, but no showers. Beginners will find the hike much easier than the long snorkel even on a calm day.

GETTING THERE   *Going south on Highway 31, turn right on Wailea Iki Drive. At the Wailea Shopping Village, turn left on Wailea Alanui Road and continue south for four miles. This is the old parking lot and is the one closest to the snorkeling. There is a larger parking lot at the next exit to the south. On the beach side of the parking lot, you will see a wide path marked "Makena State Park" and it takes you down a shady path directly to the beach, about 180 yards* (see map, page 75).

SAILFIN TANG

Fish Psychology 101

"Many fish are swimming right up and giving me dopey fish looks, which basically translate to the following statement: "Food?" That's what fish do all the time–they swim around going: "Food?" You can almost see the little questions marks over their heads. The only other thought they seem capable of is: "Yikes!"

Fish are not known for their SAT scores. This may be why they tend to do their thinking in large groups. You'll see a squadron of them coming toward you, their molecule-size brains working away on the problem ("Food?" "Food?" "Food?" "Food?"); and then you suddenly move your arm, triggering a Nuclear Fish Reaction ("Yikes!" "Yikes!" "Yikes!" "Yikes!") and FWOOOSSHH they're outta there, trailing a stream of exclamation marks."

–Dave Barry

'AHIHI BAY

This gem is a beautiful tiny bay with clear water and lots to see – even a large eel close to shore to awe the little kids. Entry is a bit slippery from the old concrete boat ramp at the far right, so sit down and work your way in carefully.

The bay itself is quite calm and shallow (5-15' deep) and the reef extends far out. This bay has a wonderful variety within a small space, so it is well worth the drive even if you're staying in the north. Another must see!

Beginners can have a great time close to shore where there are plenty of large and varied fish. More advanced snorkelers can venture out beyond into the larger bay. This is actually a tiny bay within a large, protected area. It has too much coral and rock to be a good swimming spot. Snorkel any direction. It's all fascinating snorkeling, but has no facilities and only a tiny, rocky beach.

We saw huge parrotfish, all sorts of butterflyfish and tangs, Moorish idols, triggerfish, wrasses and much more, like a large aquarium, but from the inside. Out further to the left we saw an octopus and some beautiful coral. If it's calm enough, swim way out to the left. The right side is good too.

GETTING THERE   *Going south on Highway 31, take the Wailea-Iki Drive turnoff to the right toward the hotels* (see map, page 61). *Then turn left on Wailea Alanui Road. Note the mileage at this intersection in order to determine the location of several of these beaches. 'Ahihi Bay is 5.3 miles south on this road. The road will continue south eventually crossing bare lava, but still an adequate road.*

First you'll see walls surrounding some lovely (and expensive) homes. Then at 'Ahihi Bay, you'll see the tiny bay on your right as the road narrows to one lane and curves left, skirting the tiny bay. You'll also see some houses and trees here (see map, page 79). *Park along the road wherever there is space. If parking happens to fill, there is a parking lot just .2 mile further south.*

Enter the water on the far right of the bay, only ten feet from the road. The old concrete ramp provides a little slide into the water. The beach itself is rocky rather than sandy and quite small. Just so you're sure this is the right place – you'll see stone walls and a telephone pole marked T5 just before the bay.

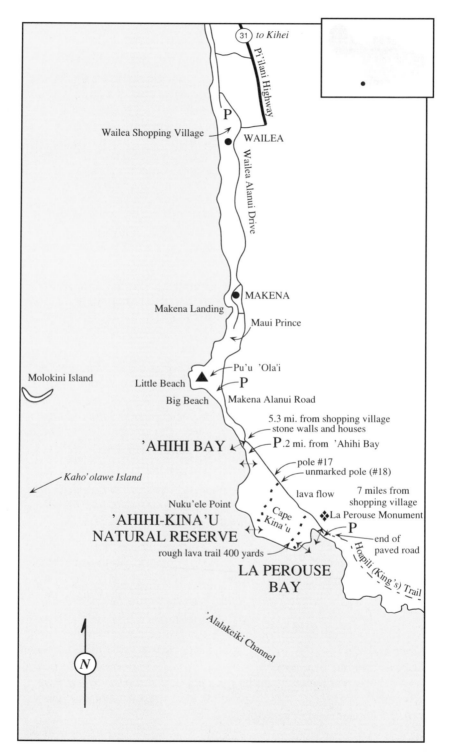

31 to Kihei

Pi'ilani Highway

P

Wailea Shopping Village

WAILEA

Wailea Alanui Drive

MAKENA

Makena Landing

Maui Prince

Molokini Island

Pu'u 'Ola'i

Little Beach

P

Big Beach

Makena Alanui Road

5.3 mi. from shopping village
stone walls and houses

'AHIHI BAY

P .2 mi. from 'Ahihi Bay

pole #17
unmarked pole (#18)

Kaho'olawe Island

lava flow

7 miles from
shopping village

Nuku'ele Point

La Perouse Monument

'AHIHI-KINA'U
NATURAL RESERVE

Cape
Kina'u

P

end of
paved road

rough lava trail 400 yards

LA PEROUSE
BAY

Hoapili (King's) Trail

'Alalakeiki Channel

N

'AHIHI BAY PARKING LOT

You'll find a parking lot just beyond 'Ahihi Bay (part of the 'Ahihi-Kina'u Natural Reserve, but there is no sign). This is a large, excellent spot for experienced snorkelers, but not really best for beginners (unless it is unusually calm) or swimmers since entry is a bit difficult and there's little sand. There's plenty of space in the dirt parking lot, but you must hike down a somewhat rocky path with little shade until you reach the beach. Shoes are a must here.

Snorkeling is uncrowded and excellent with great views of Haleakala in the background and Molokini Island out to sea. Be sure to lift your head out of the water now and then to enjoy the fabulous views towards shore. You'll want to try this one more than once, because it offers such a large area to explore.

We saw turtles, eels, colorful coral, schools of raccoon butterflyfish, scrawled filefish, bird wrasses, sailfin tang, frogfish and a huge school of Heller's barracuda (just as we entered the water).

GETTING THERE   *Go .2 mile past 'Ahihi Bay and turn right, parking in this open area* (see map, page 81). *The path starts straight toward the water and angles to the left until it reaches the rocky beach (about 200 yards of relatively easy path – compared to the lava on both sides). At the beach, continue another 100 yards south across the gravel beach to just before the next little point where entry is easier over a bit of sand.*

There's a nice shady spot to leave your stuff and you'll find the entry easier than it appears from a distance. Once out in the bay, snorkel to the right near shore as well as further out to see the variety. Our favorite spot is off the point about halfway to 'Ahihi Bay. Getting out is quite easy as long as you make sure to return to the same spot. If you prefer a one-way snorkel, swim all the way into 'Ahihi Bay and take the short hike to your car. Of course, this one-way snorkel works best if you wear booties rather than shoes that must be retrieved or carried along. We highly recommend this snorkel if you can manage it.

SPOTTED BOXFISH

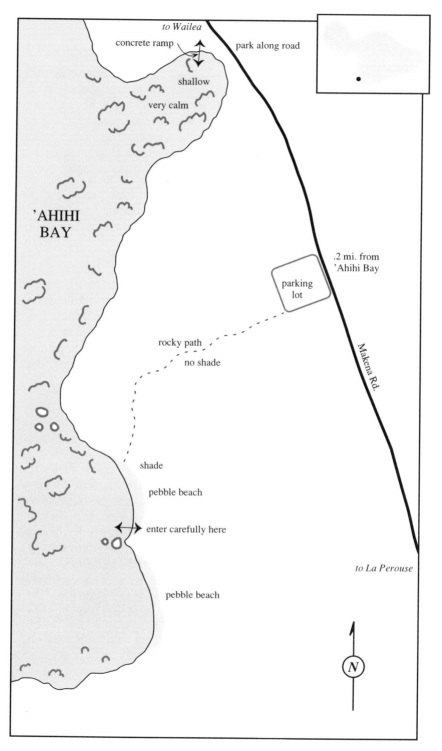

to Wailea

concrete ramp

park along road

shallow

very calm

'AHIHI
BAY

.2 mi. from
'Ahihi Bay

parking
lot

rocky path

no shade

shade

pebble beach

enter carefully here

to La Perouse

pebble beach

Makena Rd.

N

'AHIHI-KINA'U RESERVE

'Ahihi-Kina'u Natural Area Reserve is quite a large area, with one marked path that leads to a snorkeling site. It's another excellent spot, uncrowded, with room to explore, although you must hike over a sharp lava path to reach it. Reef shoes or tennis shoes are absolutely necessary on this path. It's a bare and rugged, but beautiful 400 yard hike – although not at all steep. Watch the trail carefully, because you don't want to wander out onto the open lava.

Entry is from smooth lava rock at the end of the trail, but it's not difficult if you take it slow and careful. This is usually a very calm, well-protected spot. When waves kick up at other beaches, it can be a bit murky here in spite of looking perfectly calm. The water tends to be more clear as you head out a bit.

It's crucial to leave something like a brightly-colored bag where you enter, making it easier to snorkel your way back to the right place. You'll definitely require the path to get back to your car. For snorkeling, wander in any direction as long as you stay within the protected area.

This site has plenty of variety of fish, turtles, eels, etc., but the coral isn't spectacular. The Reserve was quite murky when we've been there, so we had to snorkel out beyond the small cove before we could see much.

GETTING THERE   *Driving south on Highway 31, turn right on Wailea-Iki Dr. toward the Wailea Shopping Village (see* map, page 61). *Then turn left on Wailea Alanui Road, and be sure to note your mileage at this intersection. Continue south even after the road heads across the bare lava. Pass the little 'Ahihi Bay at 5.3 miles. At 6.8 miles from the "resort intersection" you'll see the 'Ahihi-Kina'u sign (see* map, page 79). *Park along the road. The telephone pole at the trail is #24.*

Take the trail toward the water for about 400 yards over rough lava. Wear close-toed shoes and stay on the trail. This is not the place for trying impromptu shortcuts. The trail will eventually end at the little protected bay where you can enter safely (just watch out for slippery rocks). You might have the entire bay to yourselves.

Watch your entry point carefully, because you will want to come out at exactly the same place in order to end up back on the trail. Wear a hat and bring water, too, because there's little shade here and no facilities.

'AHIHI-KINA'U UNMARKED TRAIL

This trail isn't easy to spot and requires a 500-yard hike across the lava field. However, it leads to excellent snorkeling and picnicking at a beautiful, secluded cove. A small peninsula protects this cove from most waves, so it is unusually calm and clear. This is a charming place to enjoy a great snorkel, then a quiet bag lunch.

It is definitely worth the hike, but you must wear closed-toed shoes to protect your feet from the sharp lava. Bring sunglasses, water and a hat too, since the trail is quite exposed. No facilities of any sort are available here.

GETTING THERE   *Driving south on Highway 31, turn right on Wailea-Iki Drive toward the Wailea Shopping Village* (see map, page 61). *At the shopping village, head left on Wailea Alanui Road. Continue past 'Ahihi Bay, which is 5.3 miles from this corner. Less than a mile past the bay, you'll see telephone pole #17. Watch for the next telephone pole, which probably is #18, but isn't marked* (see map, page 79). *The unmarked trail to the water starts right here. Parking is available at small turnouts about 150 yards in either direction. You'll be able to recognize the trail by small splashes of white paint. Follow this trail very carefully all the way to the water, where entry is quite easy from a pebble beach.*

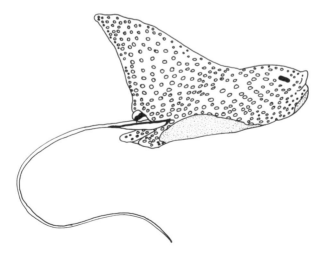

SPOTTED EAGLE RAY

LA PEROUSE BAY

At La Perouse Bay, even slight surf or swell can make entry tricky because it's rocky and slippery. Try it only in the morning when completely calm. This happens to be a local hangout, where tourists aren't necessarily appreciated. However, it's still part of the Reserve (to the right) and offers good snorkeling. It can also be fairly murky at times, so check local conditions before trying this spot. Beginners would be much better off at 'Ahihi Bay.

GETTING THERE   *Driving south on Highway 31, take the Wailea-Iki turnoff towards the big resorts* (see map, page 61). *Then turn left on Wailea Alanui Road and note the mileage at this intersection in front of the Wailea Shopping Village. Continue south as the road gets smaller and crosses bare lava. Pass the little bay and pass the 'Ahihi-Kina'u sign* (see map, page 79). *At exactly 7 miles south of the intersection, you'll come to the end of the road, for non-4WD vehicles at least. You can go a little further with the right vehicle.*

On your left will be the La Perouse Memorial monument. Just past the monument on the right is the beach with parking. Usually people are fishing or hanging out here.

OVAL BUTTERFLYFISH

Disposable Underwater Cameras

Cheap, widely available, even on the boats, and fun to use. Keep your expectations realistic, and you won't end up disappointed.

You won't get pictures like you see in National Geographic. The professionals who get all those great shots use camera setups worth $10,000 and more. They also have assistants to hold the lights, guides, spare cameras already underwater, large film budgets, and much patience. In light of all this, their books start to look like a bargain compared with trying to get these pictures all by yourself. Be sure to check out the great selection of marine life books in Maui bookstores.

Still, it's fun to try for that cute shot of your sweetie in a bikini, clowning with the fish. If you're lucky, you'll actually have identifiable fish in a few shots. The cameras won't focus closer than about 4', so the fish will look much smaller than you remember them. They work best when it's sunny with good visibility, with the subject fish as close as the camera allows.

They do work OK above the water, too, and make a great knock-around camera to haul around wet or dry, without paranoia about theft, saltwater, or damage. Try a picture of the beautiful hills of Maui as you float in the waters of 'Ahihi Bay.

MOLOKINI ISLAND

Molokini Island has become something of a legend. One might say it has almost become famous for being famous, almost a mythical destination. It is certainly heavily advertised and promoted as a fantastic snorkeling spot. There's truth in this, but it's hard to separate the reality from the hype. How good is it, really?

Molokini is indeed an amazing and interesting place, well worth visiting. Hurricane damage to the coral has left expanses of dead coral, and hence smaller fish counts. Still, the snorkeling is good, visibility almost always excellent and getting there takes you on a beautiful trip along the coast of Maui. This is also an excellent site for beginners and children. Most folks love their Molokini trip.

There are large numbers of excursions to choose from, so select your departure point, type of boat (if that's important to you), and a quality trip, if you care about the food, if you plan to dive or Snuba, or if you're a beginner and want good supervision and help. We didn't see as many fish or nearly as much coral as we had expected (the hype had given us unrealistic expectations), but the variety of fish was excellent. We did happen to see lots of eels. If you're very lucky, you might see a manta or shark, but it's not likely. It can be somewhat choppy here even on the inside, since it's almost open ocean. Your excursion can offer life vests, inner tubes, or whatever it takes to make the experience easier. The inside of the crater has little coral on the floor, but plenty of large, almost tame fish.

Although there are often more than 20 boats lined up inside the crater, there is plenty of room for everyone. Once you're in the water snorkeling, it doesn't seem crowded unless you stay near the boat. We did see plenty of butterflyfish, bird wrasses, parrotfish, Moorish idols, tangs, triggerfish, eels – the usual Maui suspects.

For an unusual experience, tag along with a dive boat to see the dramatic back side, with its sheer cliffs. The back can have strong currents, so often is beyond the abilities of even the best swimmers. Carefully supervised drift dives are the best way to see the back side. For snorkeling, the back is similar in terms of coral and fish (though you're looking mainly at a wall). It's completely uncrowded and even more dramatic in some ways, though more limited in area. Do not attempt to swim there from the front side!

Most of the better excursions (see our next chapter) stop at another site on the way back, so that you have a chance to see two sites. Five Graves/Caves is often the second site (*see page 70*).

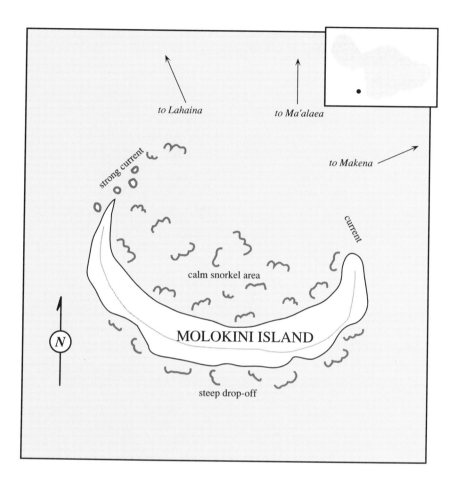

to Lahaina

to Ma'alaea

to Makena

strong current

calm snorkel area

current

N

MOLOKINI ISLAND

steep drop-off

GETTING THERE   *Numerous boat excursions leave early each morning from both Ma'alaea Harbor and the Lahaina pier. Some claim to be faster, but it makes little difference. You get out to sea and the race is on with most arriving at roughly the same time. Choose departure location according to your convenience, since they all leave so early.*

Parking is a bit easier at Ma'alaea, where you can find parking space near the pier and can drive right up to any boat.

In Lahaina there are several lots near the harbor charging about $5/day for parking, but you can drive about 1/4 mile south on Front Street to the free public parking lot. Watch for it on your left. At both harbors, you can drop passengers and gear near the boat, so one of you can check in while another parks (see Lahaina map, page 89 or Ma'alaea map, page 93).

WATER EXCURSIONS

TRILOGY

This first-rate company has five new catamarans and employs them to run excursions to Molokini from Ma'alaea Harbor (*see map, page 93*), to Lana'i from Lahaina Harbor (*see map, page 89*), Lana'i excursions from the Manele Bay Resort, and others planned for the future. They can also include overnight stays in Lana'i.

Despite the old saying, you **don't** always get what you pay for in life. But you seldom get something great without paying for it, so that's closer to the truth. These are top-of-the-line excursions and priced accordingly. But they really do know how to do it well, and you'll enjoy any of the Trilogy excursions, if you can afford them.

All excursions begin with coffee, tea, cocoa, fruit, juice and their own home-style cinnamon rolls. Various soft drinks fill the coolers for you to help yourself. Alcoholic drinks aren't served, but you may bring your own and keep it in their cooler. Lunches, whether grilled on board or on shore, usually include their delicious marinated chicken, which is addictive and memorable.

MANTA RAY

Scuba is available at an additional $45 charge and introductory dives at $55. Crew members seem happy, helpful, and quite hard-working. They manage to create an understated, yet deluxe experience, casual but impeccably detailed.

Trilogy is only allowed to use the Hulopo'e Bay beach on weekdays. On weekends and holidays, Trilogy runs a Lana'i trip called "Seafari". You sail along the south side of Lana'i to snorkel at Cathedrals or Shark Fin Rock. Then back to the Manele Bay Harbor for lunch and an island tour if you wish.

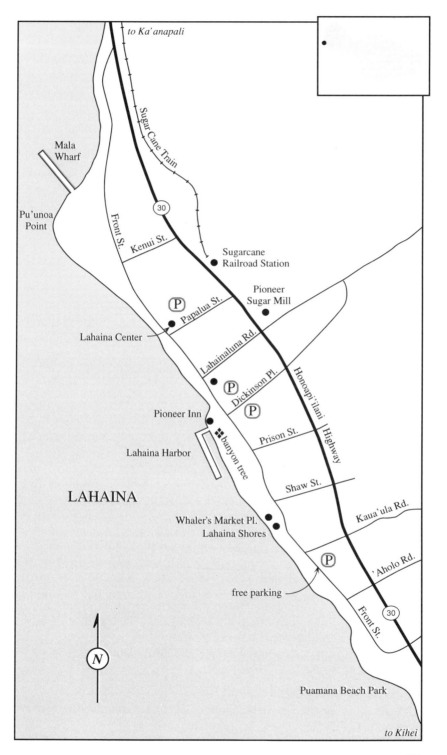

to Ka'anapali

Sugar Cane Train

Mala Wharf

Pu'unoa Point

Front St.

Kenui St.

30

Sugarcane Railroad Station

Pioneer Sugar Mill

(P)

Papalua St.

Lahaina Center

Lahainaluna Rd.

(P)

Dickinson Pl.

(P)

Honoapi'ilani Highway

Pioneer Inn

Prison St.

banyon tree

Lahaina Harbor

Shaw St.

LAHAINA

Kaua'ula Rd.

Whaler's Market Pl.
Lahaina Shores

'Aholo Rd.

(P)

free parking

Front St.

30

N

Puamana Beach Park

to Kihei

89

The catamarans are beautiful, although be prepared for little shade on all except Trilogy I. They always attempt to sail at least part of the way, although this can be slow if the wind is light. They have alternative sites for days when the weather is unfavorable, and are well-organized, so you don't have to worry about a thing. Everyone seems to have a good time. See the section on Lana'i for more information about these destinations.

The Molokini trip costs $75 plus tax for an adult. Lahaina to Lana'i is $149. A shorter trip for Lana'i hotel guests to Cathedrals or Shark Fin Cove is $85. Children ages 3-12 are half price; under 3 go for free. Trilogy does not offer coupons or discounts.
800-874-2666, 661-4743, fax 667-7766. (The area code for HI is 808)

NAVATEK II

This large and comfortable ship cruises over to the Lana'i site Cathedrals easily in two hours from Lahaina Harbor. The ship rides quite high in the water on its special pontoons, and is remarkably smooth. It leaves promptly at 8:45 a.m. and returns at 2:45, providing a delightful opportunity to snorkel a wonderful site and fully enjoy the trip as well. It holds 149 people, so it's best if you like lots of company.

One of Navatek's specialties is a hot breakfast, featuring lavish waffles with strawberries, whipped cream and much more, served buffet-style in the main cabin. After a decent interval to eat, the crew members are introduced and various activities explained. This is somewhat more like a cruise ship event, as they let you in on all the activities and personnel available, including naturalist, photographer, Scuba, Snuba, Hawai'ian crafts, tales of Lana'i history and legends, and even massage ($15 for 15 minutes). You can watch the excellent video, check out the fish ID books, or laze in the sun or shade up on the large deck with plenty of lounge chairs. Head right on out there if long orientations aren't your cup of tea.

Leaving Maui we were immediately treated to the sight of three bottlenose dolphins swimming and leaping just inches in front of the boat as we sped along. Cruising by Lana'i, we saw numerous little flying fish near the boat. The rugged cliffs you travel under are most impressive.

Snuba

Snuba was developed as a simpler alternative to Scuba for shallow dives in resort conditions. Because Snuba divers are strictly limited in depth and conditions, and always accompanied by an instructor, training takes just 15-30 minutes. Two people share a small inflatable raft, which holds a Scuba air tank. A 20' hose leads from the tank to a light harness on each diver. A soft, light weight belt completes your outfit. Very light and tropical!

Once in the water, your instructor teaches you to breathe through your regulator (which has a mouthpiece just like your snorkel) on the surface until you're completely comfortable. You're then free to swim around as you like (only down to 20' deep, of course). The raft will automatically follow you as you tour the bay.

It's that easy! You have to be at least eight years old, and have normal good health. Kids do well, and it is so simple that senior citizens often give it a try.

We are certified Scuba divers, yet we tried Snuba because this was a perfect place to see what made it special. It actually has some advantages over Scuba in that you're free of the cumbersome equipment. There's none of the macho attitude you sometimes see on dive boats.

Snuba strikes us as a fun, reasonably safe experience if you pay attention and use it according to directions. Where the reef is shallow, and conditions calm, it can actually be better than diving because you're so unencumbered in the water.

Warning: *pay attention* to the instructions, because even at these shallow depths, you must know the proper way to surface. You must remember to **never** hold your breath as you ascend, or you could force a bubble of air into your blood. Breathing out continually while surfacing is not intuitive, but absolutely necessary when you're breathing compressed air. This is especially important to remember if you're used to surface diving where you always hold your breath.

Enjoy, and dive safely!

We had a full hour and a half, excellent snorkel at the Cathedrals site, where we saw octopus, eels, peacock flounder, saddleback butterflyfish, and much more. Cathedrals lies along the sheer cliffs of southern Lana'i, quite a spectacular setting.

As is often the case on large boats, Scuba and Snuba people entered the water first from the easy steps, so snorkelers get to wait unless they are willing and able to jump in from the side. Restrooms were larger, cleaner and more numerous than on smaller boats. A warm water shower after snorkeling was wonderful, making it possible to change out of salty clothes and be even more comfortable for the trip back to Maui.

Snuba costs an extra $45 and is available for ages eight and up. The video is excellent quality and costs $32. Better than usual underwater cameras are $27. Donna, the naturalist, was knowledgeable and always available to help. She brought along plenty of interesting books, exhibits and other information.

Lunch is buffet-style, and includes chicken, hamburgers, pasta, salad with sodas and alcoholic drinks of all sorts readily available throughout the trip. Cookies and ice cream on the return voyage complete the picture. If your style is "one of each, please", you'll wind up more than satisfied: stuffed and sozzled, too.

Our only complaint (as advanced snorkelers and curious wanderers) was that they set boundaries rather close, guarded by crew on surfboards, and granted no exemptions. It was all in the name of safety, as there was a pretty good surge near the rocks, but it felt overly rigid, and could make you feel a little herded.

This is one of the more expensive trips available, but it's a great one as long as a cheery party cruise ship atmosphere is what you're looking for. This trip will cost $135 for an adult (including tax), $67.50 for ages 5-12. Their dinner cruise on Maui costs $90.24 for an adult, $47.78 for a child. Both are available any day except Sunday. 661-8787

RACCOON BUTTERFLYFISH

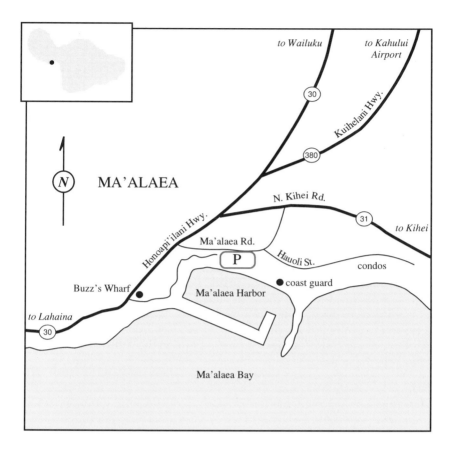

EXPEDITIONS FERRY

The Lahaina-Lana'i passenger ferry, called "Expeditions", offers five trips each way per day from Lahaina Harbor to Manele Harbor on Lana'i. Fares are $50 round trip for adults; $40 for children 2-11; under 2, free on your lap. The small, enclosed ferry takes about 45 minutes. They can add car, jeep, golf or overnight stay in Lana'i to the package. Bring lots of paper or plastic money if you plan on staying, as there are no inexpensive options other than camping.

You can also create your own delightful day trip by walking just 10 minutes to the beach in front of the Manele Bay Hotel. Take a picnic lunch or splurge at the Manele Bay Resort. Facilities such as inside showers, restrooms, water, shade, and picnic tables are all available on the beach and at the harbor. For more details about this destination, see our section about Lana'i, page 111. 661-3756

CLUB LANA'I

This unusual excursion takes about 150 people to an eight-acre, somewhat funky resort, one of the few parcels of independently-owned land on Lana'i, and a moderate cost alternative.

Departures are from Lahaina Harbor. Nothing fancy here, no pretense, no luxury promised or given, and no excuses. A good old working class excursion here: plenty of regulation donuts, certified to exceed minimum fat and sugar standards set by the Peace Officers Association, and coffee in plastic cups await on boarding.

The well-worn boat departs on time at 7:30 a.m.. This is unusual on Maui, where departures are more often anywhere from kind of late to unbelievably late (especially annoying if the operators insisted you get up before dawn and check in early for their convenience). Club Lana'i runs a big boat, pretty plain, but with plenty of reasonably comfortable bench seating inside and sun on top for the easy cruise nine miles over to the near side of Lana'i. After docking, you must attend an onshore briefing.

Then it's back to the boat if you'd like to snorkel because the reef is too shallow near shore. They take two snorkeling trips out (just minutes from shore) to a nice healthy reef with some turtles, lots of fish, canyons, and some of the largest and healthiest coral reef in Hawai'i. Scuba is available for an extra charge. Swim out away from the crowd and it's very pleasant. Beginners may find it a bit choppy some days (like Molokini can be), but there's plenty of clearance since the reef here is from ten to twenty feet beneath the surface. This puts you a little farther from the coral and fish than we prefer on a rough day, however. In calm conditions, you can swim in to the more shallow reef area. Visibility is generally not quite as good as on the more rocky far side of Lana'i.

On shore, there's a no-frills but hearty lunch served buffet-style, with unlimited free drinks at the bar. Free recreational gear includes popular plastic kayaks that are very easy to handle in the calm shallow water, and bikes for touring (not an exciting ride though, just a hot, sandy and dusty road along the shore).

Club Lana'i does have a very broad white sand beach with shade, hammocks, beach chairs, and nice swimming if you like shallow water – just right for small children. They have lots of hammocks, but people tend to claim them early by tossing in their stuff, so grab yours early too, if you want to lie around. Other activities include a history tour, weaving demonstration, nature walk, volleyball, horse shoes, even massage (extra charge). There is a small store in case you forgot something.

Motion sickness

Motion sickness ("seasickness or carsickness") is a minor inner ear disorder which can really cut into your pleasure on the water, on long, curvy road trips, or in choppy air. Fortunately, motion sickness is quite controllable these days. All it takes is a little advance planning to turn a potentially miserable experience into a normal, fun one. Don't let old fears keep you from great water adventures anymore.

Mel can get seasick just by vividly imagining a rocking boat, so he's tried just about every remedy personally. These field trials are a messy business, so we'll spare you the details, and just pass on what really works in our experience.

Forget the wrist pressure-point bands – they don't do the job for anyone we've ever met. You might as well put them in the closet along with your ultrasonic pest repeller, in our opinion. We're open to reports from anyone who has made fair trials and really gets relief this way.

Scopolamine, a time-release prescription ear patch, has been on the market and is reputed to be quite effective. There are some possible side effects we'd rather not experience. So for the time being, we personally avoid patches. We've had reliable reports from folks who use and have had absolutely no problems with Scopolamine, so it could be right for you.

The most effective remedy we've found so far is Meclizine, a pill available by prescription only, to be taken four times daily. It works perfectly for Mel, with no noticeable side effects. Alcohol can interact with it to make you drowsy, but a glass of wine at dinner doesn't knock Mel out. We learned about it when Jon Carroll, a columnist in the San Francisco Chronicle, reported that it had sufficed for him in 15-25' swells on the way to Antarctica. If it does the job there, it should handle all but the most radical of snorkeling excursions. Write us if you've snorkeled Cape Horn, and aren't currently institutionalized.

An alternative that works pretty well is Benadryl, usually used as a decongestant, available over the counter. It is also effective against motion sickness. Mel discovered this accidentally when he used Benadryl before a rough night dive, and felt great.

Use these medicines carefully, and only after consulting your doctor. In some cases, you must avoid alcohol, other drugs, or diving, since some medicines can produce drowsiness.

Club Lana'i is a great casual family alternative, and a bit easier on the budget than the luxury excursions. Not elegant or secluded, but rather an enjoyable campy kind of action-filled day with plenty of time to get happily worn out. And you can watch the excellent video in the cabin on the way back or tan more up top. Club Lana'i charges $89 plus tax per adult, $29 for ages 4-12, $69 for ages 13-20. 871-1144

NAUTILUS

A glassbottom/side boat (which they describe as semi-submersible; not a submarine) boarding from Lahaina Harbor (slip #10). Rates vary from $30-$45 per adult, depending on whether you get a discount coupon. The large windows wrap under and to the side allowing a wide view. With an excellent narrative, this offers a chance to learn about the underwater world without getting wet. Since you stay on the surface, if you're prone to motion sickness, you may need medication on days with a good swell.*(see Motion Sickness, page 95)*. 667-2133

ATLANTIS

This submarine trip also leaves from the Lahaina Harbor. Check in at the Pioneer Inn on Front Street directly across from the pier. The view is through portholes, because this is a real submarine, which takes you down to 100' deep. This depth will run you $69 per adult and takes about two hours, because you need to take a boat trip out to board the sub. The submarine ride itself lasts about 45 minutes. 667-2224

SEAHORSE

PRIDE OF MAUI

Located at Ma'alaea Harbor, ready to sprint for Molokini. This is a sleek and speedy 65' catamaran with indoor space for seating and gear, but lots more room on the sunny, upper deck where all the activities center.

A charming and high-energy local entertainer who goes by the name of Eddee (not a misprint, this guy is a character!) was the singer, guitar-player, "master of ceremonies" for the entire trip and really made the trip something special. Passengers and crew were on the young side. All seemed to thoroughly enjoy the day. You start out with the usual continental breakfast – in this case with a choice of muffins, fruit, coffee, and fruit punch.

The trip to Molokini is smooth and offers plenty of comfort. The crew set boundaries for snorkeling at Molokini, although weren't overly rigid about them. With so many boats anchored at once, it isn't surprising that they try hard to keep an eye on all their charges.

Lunch was ample, with a choice of chicken (which disappeared fast), huge hamburgers, grilled fish with plenty of salads, soft drinks and beer. The second site was one they called "Turtle Town" just offshore from the Maui Prince Hotel, a beautiful spot indeed. Scuba is offered for an extra $45, while Snuba is $35. At this site divers had a chance to see frogfish and the elusive green leaf scorpionfish. Depending on the weather, the second site can sometimes be off Olowalu. Both of these second sites are excellent and can be just as much fun as Molokini. All in all, a most pleasant, relaxing way to see some of the best that Maui has to offer. Pride of Maui charges $70 (including tax) per adult for the morning trip, $40 for ages 5-12, $60 for ages 13-18. The afternoon trip is only $40 per adult and $20 for ages 5-12, but offers only one stop and choppier water. This doesn't go out every day, so call first. Keep in mind that afternoon trips might be diverted to La Perouse or Coral Gardens, so (as with any excursion) try the morning if your heart is set on Molokini. 875-0955

SILENT LADY

This large "pirate" sailing ship, a two-masted square rigger complete with cannon, stands out in the crowd at the Ma'alaea harbor. This charming ship has a wood exterior and comfortable seating (padded seats and backs). The travel time to Molokini can be variable depending on the winds, so this ship departs early at 7 a.m. The crew is experienced, attentive, and helpful, so this trip has become very popular in spite of the competition from the faster boats. It can hold up to 46 people. On our trip bottlenose dolphins chose to swim with the ship to everyone's delight. They like to swim in the bow wake, just under the surface of the water, and sometimes jumping playfully out, with a thrilling display of elegant speed.

Snorkeling time at Molokini was longer than many boats offer (a good one and a half hours) because of quick, easy access into the water. On the way home, the ship sailed by Wailea (several times) to appear in the background of a TV program being filmed at the time, making for an unusual and enjoyable day.

Food was ample: continental breakfast (muffins, fruit, coffee) and lunch (deli sandwiches – teriyaki, tuna, chicken), and big cookies for dessert. Chips and drinks are provided, but no alcohol. This ship offers more personal attention than most and would certainly be the one to select if you enjoy the romantic notion of old-fashioned sailing. A second snorkeling site is usually visited on the way home. Most of the boats troll from the back on each trip, but this was the first time we saw them catch anything – a big mahi mahi. Be sure to take medication if you're prone to seasickness, as this boat rocks and rolls. Silent Lady charges $66.95 plus tax per adult and $39.95 for ages 2-11. Specials are sometimes available when booked directly. 875-1112

SOUTH PACIFIC KAYAKS

Kayaking adventures, as well as kayak rentals (with attachment for your car), sales (T-shirts to kayaks) and hiking trips. Getting to the snorkeling by kayak is both pleasant and offers a chance to snorkel hard-to-reach spots.

The "Marine Reserve Explorer" trip (their longest snorkeling trip) is small (maximum eight persons) making it far more personal than most boat excursions. This trip costs $85. Meet at 6:30 a.m. at the office in Kihei near Denny's where their van will transport you to the start. Confirm first, though, because weather conditions can call for a change of time or place. Another van will bring the kayaks.

Choose either a single or double kayak and it will be waiting, along with life vests. These are stable, quality molded plastic kayaks, not the sleek ultra-expensive ones made for speed. Gear can be attached to your kayak, but put it in one or two bags, as loose stuff isn't easy to transport. South Pacific Kayaks supplies snorkeling gear if needed (optical lenses if requested ahead of time) and has dry storage available for cameras. Booties are required, but they can supply them. Instructions are good and everything is well-organized. After ten minutes of practice, you'll be ready to go. As their guide likes to say, "no worries."

On their longest trip, there are several stops, usually starting at La Perouse, then heading for "The Aquarium" in the Ahihi Kina'u Marine Reserve. This would be very difficult to reach by land and is an excellent snorkeling spot. It was clearer than close to shore and we had a chance to see an octopus, dolphins, and rays (but no whales this trip). The second stop was "The Fish Pond", a little bay protected by the breakwater, making it perfect for beginning snorkelers. Lunch was served here on the beach (huge deli sandwiches, cookies, and sodas). There was time to hike around a bit to enjoy this beautiful site. The third stop was Ahihi Bay, another excellent, easy snorkeling site with turtles in residence.

Each kayaking stint was fairly short and easy, only about fifteen minutes, although could take much longer in bad weather. The hardest part was lifting the kayaks in and out of the water, walking on lava, arduous even with the guide's help. Be sure to tell them if you can't help with this. Since the group is small and the guide is patient, timing is relaxed. This trip lasted till 3 p.m. Don't underestimate how much sun you will get while out on the water like this, and come prepared!

Remember to bring SPF1000 sunscreen, T-shirt, broad-brimmed hat and sunglasses. This is certainly a unique, quiet, delightful way to see some of Maui's best snorkeling sites. Even when only two people are going, they still won't cancel a trip, unless high seas interfere. Office in Kihei at 2439 S. Kihei Rd. in the Rainbow Mall. 875-4848, (800) 776-2326, fax 875-4691, kayak@maui.net

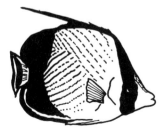

THREADFIN BUTTERFLYFISH

SNORKEL MAUI

Ann Fielding and Sue Robinson provide individualized, informative snorkeling tours from land. Call to check when the next trip is scheduled or make your own arrangements with them. They take a maximum of 6 people and cater to your particular needs and abilities. Tell them if you are a beginner or plan to bring children because they can have special equipment available.

You rendezvous at the Wailea Shopping Village, and join them in their van, or follow if you wish. Sites vary depending on local weather and waves. They escort you to special sites they know well and can take you to see fish friends of theirs that hang out in specific spots.

The day we joined Sue, her first site choice led us to park in the parking lot just south of 'Ahihi Bay. Shoes or booties are required for the short hike down to the beach *(see map, page 81)*. We sat in a beautiful and secluded spot at the edge of the rocky beach, learning about the geology of the Hawai'ian islands as well as reef building and the story of Hawai'ian coral and fish. She then led us on a guided snorkeling tour of the area, pointing out such beauties as male and female bird wrasses, oval butterflyfish, Heller's barracuda, razor coral, a white-mouth moral, blue-stripe butterflyfish, fantail tang, and more.

Our second stop was the little park at the south end of the Maui Prince Hotel *(see map, page 71)*, where we relaxed with muffins and juice before another guided snorkel to see some of the many turtles and fish at this reef.

This is a wonderful and most unusual opportunity to have far more personal attention than any of the tour boats can provide. Sue and Ann can help you learn to use your gear, teach you to differentiate the kinds of Hawai'ian coral, or simply provide a safe and fun way to introduce children to the precious resources of Hawai'ian reefs. Their emphasis is on education and tailoring the experience to each person's unique interests. 879-3584, (800) 635-1273.

Be Careful Out There!

PADI and NAUI attempt to regulate the diving industry with strict rules, since there are serious risks involved. No one is allowed to dive without certification (a "C" card) or at least phone verification of status. Anyone who wants to dive without proper training is certainly a fool, and the shops who will take such rash people out are equally foolish. But it happens every day.

We have seen excursions all over the world offering to take people down without proof of certification. This is not the mark of the highest level of safety consciousness, so keep in mind that other advice and services from such operators may be similarly casual. Always take extra care with any rental equipment.

Especially when business is slow, it's hard to resist taking divers (or snorkelers) to sites they can't handle. At least on the good snorkeling excursions, they usually keep a close eye on all their charges, so it can be like having a lifeguard along.

With a dive boat you may find yourself on the surface as a snorkeler in much rougher conditions than the divers 60' beneath you. Be your own lifeguard and have a buddy!

ED ROBINSON DIVING ADVENTURES

Ed is the owner and organizer of this highly individualized, competent dive operation, as well as a professional undersea photographer. They don't encourage snorkelers though, since that would limit their choices of sites. Two of his boats with captain and crew typically meet at the Kihei boat ramp at 6:30 a.m. for an early start to catch the best conditions. This is between Kihei and Wailea *(see map, page 61)*. Restrooms, shower, and ample parking are available here.

As they quickly launch the boats, you have coffee and donuts while discussing the needs and interests of the group. They make every attempt to choose a site that is both appropriate for the group and new to everyone. The larger boat heads for Lana'i on Wednesdays, while the smaller one carrying only six divers heads for Molokini or any number of sites off Maui's western shore.

Thursday is a night dive, which includes dinner. An experienced guide accompanies each group, taking a bright light to point out interesting sea life. Divers may choose to stick with their buddy rather than hang with the full group if they prefer.

Pre-dive orientation on the way out is professional and individualized. Returning, it's fun to talk about what everyone has seen. If you're looking for a thorough and informative dive operation that attracts return customers, this is the one to consider.

We tried the small boat for a trip to the back side of Molokini, a beautiful drift dive where the island drops 250' with the deep blue ocean always at your side. Our second dive was off Little Beach, where we saw octopuses, lots of turtles, frog fish, leaf scorpionfish, and much more. Visibility was excellent, and the currents were slow, just right for drifting.

They recommend that you book early (preferably from home) because these trips do fill, especially in the winter.
P. O. Box 616, Kihei, Maui, HI 96753.
879-3584, (800) 635-1273

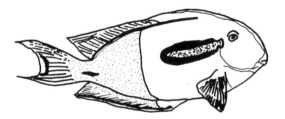

ORANGEBAND SURGEONFISH

Discounts

Discounts are available for many excursions. If you're so inclined, a little work and the right questions can save you a fair chunk of change. Begin by picking up one of the numerous free promotional magazines such as Maui Gold. These are readily available at the airport and in town. They usually include special offers, coupons and other deals to attract customers.

Calling an excursion office directly, and asking if there are any special offers can sometimes pay off, especially in the winter when things are slower. Summer and holidays the ships fill more quickly, but there is still plenty of competition on Maui, so it's always worth a try.

Ships often charge less for children and nothing for toddlers. Each ship picks its own definition of age. Don't hesitate to ask about senior discounts, repeat customer discounts, and kama'aina rate (if you live in the islands and can prove it by showing your driver's license).

For discounts ranging from 10-20%, try Activity World in Lahaina. They buy blocks of tickets and can mail tickets to the mainland. They're also open every day of the year from 7 a.m. until 9 p.m. They're located at 888 Wainee, Suite 130. Call (800) 624-7771 or 667-7777 in Maui. Last-minute tickets are also sometimes offered at an even better price. This is helpful if you are flexible, but not so useful if your vacation time is in short supply.

For a really cheap trip, sign up for a Timeshare offer. You will have to sit through an hour or two of sales talk in exchange for your bargain trip. Do not underestimate their sales ability!

When you do book tickets ahead of time and charge them to your credit card, remember that when the ship goes out with or without you, you will be charged for the trip. The fine print usually requires you to cancel at least 24 hours ahead. You may wake up to weather that doesn't suit **you** only to find that the ship sailed anyway, and you will get to pay as agreed.

Often your destination isn't guaranteed. You might have your heart set on Molokini only to find the ship change to Makena Landing due to rough weather. This does not entitle you to cancel. Keep in mind they do have to make changes for safety reasons so go with the flow.

AIR EXCURSIONS

BIPLANE TOURS

If the romance of winging through the air in a convertible plane appeals to you, consider taking a spin in the cute biplane "Naco Classic", a modern reproduction of the 1935 model. It's a charming, candy-apple red aerial confection sure to delight you.

Two passengers fit snugly up front. Although it's an open cockpit, the wing provides shade, the windshield protects you from most of the wind, earphones cut the noise a bit, and the engine provides more than enough warmth.

It departs from one of the hangers on the inland side of the Kahului Airport (*see map, page 145*). This is the same area used by the helicopters. From West Maui, take the Hana Highway south, then Kala passes the control tower and you will see the hangers. When you make your reservation, you'll be given instructions as to which hanger to meet in and how to get in the gate.

Besides the fun of an old-fashioned plane, the view of the beaches of Maui is more colorful than you might imagine from the ground. Reefs are clearly visible as you float over. A number of specific tours are offered, although you can arrange to fly wherever you prefer. The pilot provides an interesting commentary through the earphones, although the background noise sometimes interferes when you want to ask questions. A wonderful opportunity to see Maui from another perspective – and a most beautiful one at that! 878-2860

HELICOPTERS

Maui also sports several helicopter companies, each with a wide range of choices, all spectacular and all expensive. They are heavily advertised and often have specials, so watch the local tourist pamphlets. The Haleakala Crater is the big attraction, but the turquoise beaches, 'Iao Needle, West Maui Mountains, and central valley are all beautiful to see from the air. See page 95 if you're susceptible to motion sickness.

Blue Hawai'ian Helicopters: 871-8844

Hawai'i Helicopters: 877-3900

Sunshine Helicopters: 871-0722

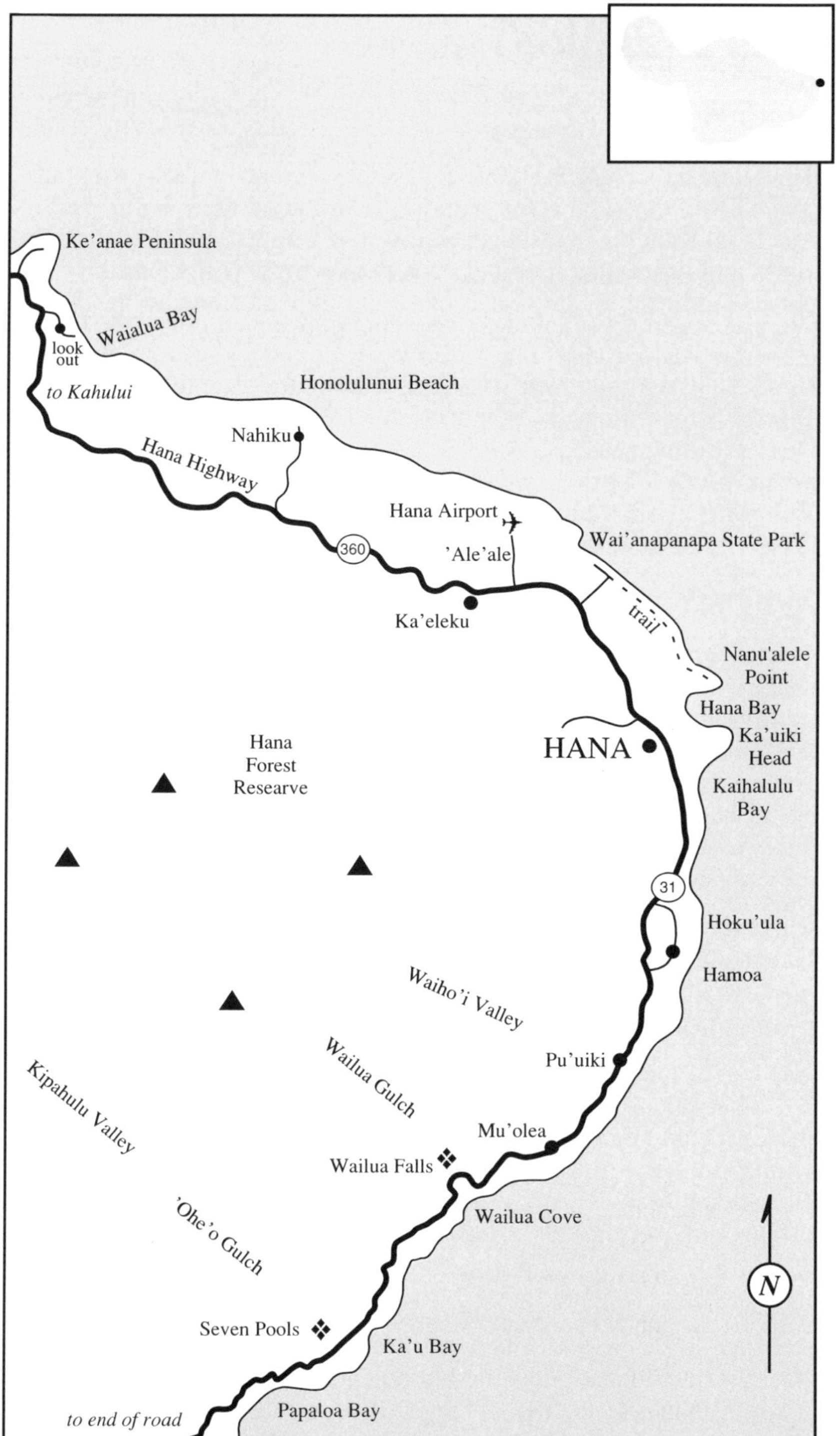
Ke'anae Peninsula
Waialua Bay
look out
to Kahului
Honolulunui Beach
Nahiku
Hana Highway
Hana Airport
360
'Ale'ale
Wai'anapanapa State Park
Ka'eleku
trail
Nanu'alele Point
Hana Bay
Ka'uiki Head
HANA
Hana Forest Researve
Kaihalulu Bay
31
Hoku'ula
Hamoa
Waiho'i Valley
Wailua Gulch
Pu'uiki
Kipahulu Valley
Mu'olea
Wailua Falls
Wailua Cove
'Ohe'o Gulch
N
Seven Pools
Ka'u Bay
Papaloa Bay
to end of road

LAND EXCURSIONS

HANA

The Hana area (*see map, page 105*) offers a wonderful day trip, but it's a LONG day. The Hana Highway takes about three hours each way from Kahului, and longer if you stop a bit to enjoy the gorgeous views and waterfalls. It's an extremely slow road with countless twists and turns, so prepare to take your time and soak in the sight of jungle greenery here on the wet side of the island.

Hana itself is a tiny town with great charm and beautiful beaches. You can snorkel here, but the west coast is preferable, so travel to Hana for other reasons. The Seven Pools (actually more like twelve) are now called by their old Hawai'ian name of 'Oheo Gulch. Waterfalls abound here, but so do tourists, so don't expect a fast drive on this extremely narrow road.

HALEAKALA CRATER

Driving up nearly to the top of Maui is one exciting way to view the sunrise (*see map, page 107*). The crater is spectacular and huge. Keep in mind that it will be quite cold at nearly 10,000' so bring warm clothing. Great hiking trails await, but the altitude takes some getting used to. Don't try too much, too soon, or you risk altitude sickness. At the first sign of any illness like headache or nausea, just head down the mountain. Going down a couple of thousand feet is all you need to quickly recover.

It has recently become exceedingly popular to bicycle down the Haleakala Highway. The road is quite narrow, so watch out for groups of bicycles. If you'd like to try this beautiful ride, there are plenty of companies offering the trip.

Ask lots of questions before settling on a company. Do they pick you up? That can be a mixed blessing if you have to get up at 3 a.m. and then get hauled around for hours for other pickups. You might save money and time by choosing a tour that has you get yourself to the cycle home base. Be sure to ask what time they actually begin biking, how large is the group, and when and where you will eat.

UPCOUNTRY

At about 3,000' you will be in the area called "upcountry" where you can ride horses, checking out an entirely different side of Maui. This is ranch country where they still raise excellent beef. It's a chance to see the real working "old west" – Maui style.

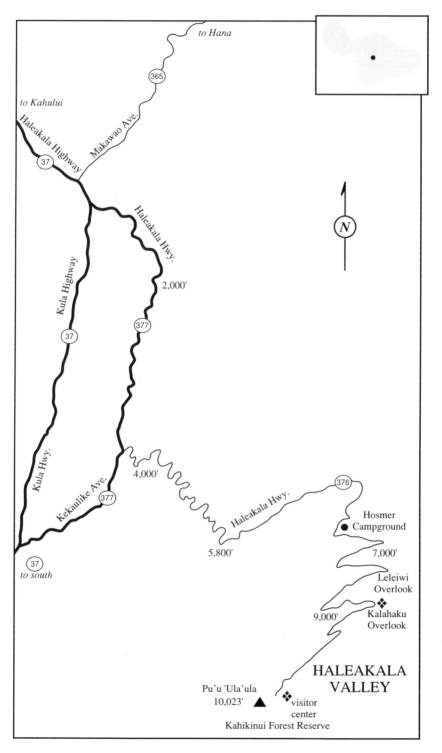

to Hana

365

to Kahului

Haleakala Highway

Makawao Ave.

37

Haleakala Hwy.

2,000'

Kula Highway

37

377

N

Kula Hwy.

Kekaulike Ave.

4,000'

377

Haleakala Hwy.

376

Hosmer Campground

5,800'

7,000'

37
to south

Leleiwi Overlook

9,000'

Kalahaku Overlook

HALEAKALA VALLEY

Pu'u 'Ula'ula
10,023' ▲

visitor center

Kahikinui Forest Reserve

107

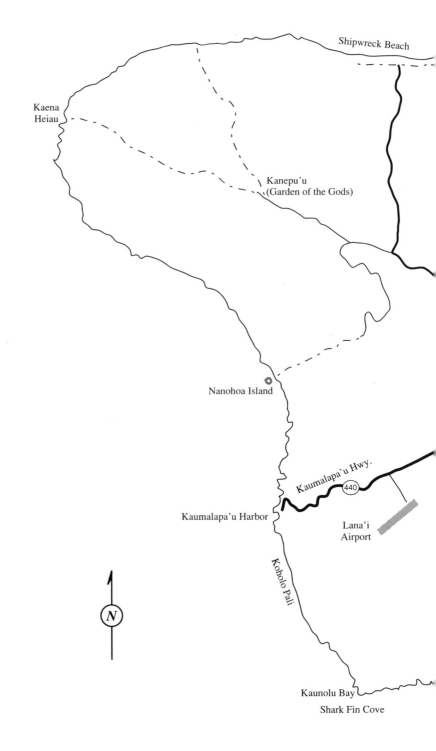

Shipwreck Beach

Kaena
Heiau

Kanepu'u
(Garden of the Gods)

Nanohoa Island

Kaumalapa'u Hwy.

440

Kaumalapa'u Harbor

Lana'i
Airport

Koholo Pali

N

Kaunolu Bay

Shark Fin Cove

LANA'I

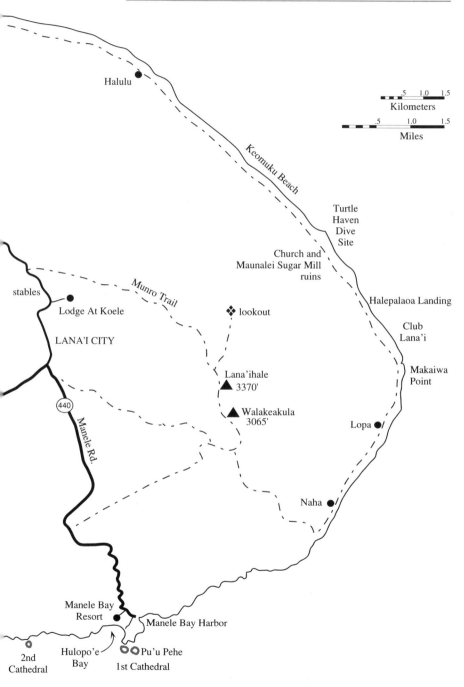

Halulu

Keomuku Beach

.5 1.0 1.5
Kilometers

.5 1.0 1.5
Miles

Turtle
Haven
Dive
Site

Church and
Maunalei Sugar Mill
ruins

stables

Munro Trail

Halepalaoa Landing

Lodge At Koele

lookout

Club
Lana'i

LANA'I CITY

Makaiwa
Point

440

Lana'ihale
3370'

Manele Rd.

Walakeakula
3065'

Lopa

Naha

Manele Bay
Resort

Manele Bay Harbor

2nd
Cathedral

Hulopo'e
Bay

Pu'u Pehe
1st Cathedral

LANA'I

For that one extra-special snorkeling experience, consider a trip to Lana'i, where beautiful Hulopo'e Bay awaits (see page 114). A day trip on the Lahaina to Lana'i ferry takes you within minutes of this famous beach, as well as several other smaller snorkeling sites.

If your time and budget allows, stay overnight at either of the two big resorts or the one small hotel in Lana'i City.

Trilogy, Navatek II and Club Lana'i each offer their own unique excursions to Lana'i (for reviews, see excursions from Maui, page 88-95). We've included our review of the ferry along with hotel information in case you'd like to visit, or better yet, stay awhile. From West Maui, the ferry is usually faster and more convenient than flying. Cars and jeeps can be rented in Lana'i City. 565-7227

EXPEDITIONS

Ferry service from Maui to Lana'i. Departs from Lahaina Harbor, directly in front of the Pioneer Inn, and arrives at the harbor at Manele Bay. $50 round trip ($40 for children 2-11). This is probably the best deal on Maui for $50.

Five trips go each day, taking about 45 minutes for the trip. The ships are quite seaworthy, and very few trips get cancelled. Departures from Lahaina at 6:45 a.m., 9:15 a.m., 12.45 p.m., 3:15 p.m., and 5:45 p.m.. Returns from Lana'i at 8:00 a.m., 10:30 a.m., 2:00 p.m., 4:30 p.m., and 6:45 p.m. Reservations are advised if you want a sure seat, and they ask that you board 15 minutes early. They do leave right on time, so confirm and don't arrive a minute late.

Expeditions I is a 40' ship, holding 36 passengers, while Expeditions II is 50', seating 64. It's a smooth, quiet ride with plenty of comfortable, padded seats inside. They serve coffee on the first departure, so even the groggy, caffeine-addicted among you can enjoy the sunrise. On the late ferry back to Maui, there is a romantic view of the lights from the little front deck.

Packages are available through Expeditions which include a car (about $100 per day), golfing ($150) and/or overnight stays on Lana'i at either the Lodge at Koele or the Manele Bay Resort ($300-500 per night plus $100 to golf). Everything on Lana'i makes Maui look like a bargain – except for the wonderful beaches, which are still free. 661-3756, P. O. Box 10, HI 96767

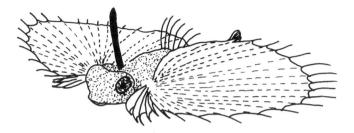

FLYING GURNARD

MANELE BAY RESORT

There is only one waterfront hotel in Lana'i, and it is exquisite.
Spread out on a small hill overlooking a large beach, the Manele
Bay Resort has the casual elegance of old money. A championship
golf course wraps around in back, providing greenery amid the arid
hillside. Rooms are large and very comfortable without being gaudy.
The hotel sprawls gracefully on several levels, and it's fun to wander
into courtyard gardens with helpful labels for identifying the exotic
selection of tropical plants. The feeling is peaceful, quiet and sub-
dued.

The staff is always friendly and they go out of their way to see that
guests have whatever help they need. Breakfast in the room arrives
at precisely the time ordered and provides an ample treat to savor on
the patio.

The outlying rooms require a hike just to the pool, then another
hike down the hill to the beach. However, vans are always out in
front of the lobby to offer transportation. Decor is tastefully
understated, dramatic yet informal, with lots of antique art objects
collected from China. The cuisine has received many outstanding
reviews. And pods of dolphins cruise the snorkeling beach.

Manele Bay Resort provides luxurious relaxation at premium prices,
$250-500 per day. Several of the best snorkeling spots on Lana'i are
within walking distance. And there's certainly enough to keep you
busy for a week. Few snorkelers would complain if heaven looked
and worked just like the Manele Bay Resort. (800) 321-4666

111

THE LODGE AT KOELE

For those who can stand being away from the beach, the stately Lodge at Koele provides a cool, green setting among Norfolk Island Pines. Up here in the hills, scenery, service and food are soothing and delightful. The Lodge also has an adjacent garden, pool, pond and golf course. Riding stables are nearby. This unique resort is worth a look even if you don't plan to stay. The lobby looks like a casual museum, with fine Asian antiques everywhere.

Each afternoon at four they serve a wonderful tea and scones, and much more, for their guests (as well as any who catch the shuttle up from the Manele Bay Resort). Of course, guests here can also take the shuttle down to the beach, leaving each half hour. Rates start at around $300 per night. (800) 321-4666

ON YOUR OWN

In Lana'i, just a 5-10 minute walk from the harbor brings you to some of the best snorkeling and swimming, at broad and beautiful Hulopo'e Bay. Showers, restrooms, shade, a beautiful wide sand beach await you. A great hotel is steps away, if you require more (like gourmet dining).

Come early, stay late and try several different snorkeling spots within easy walking distance. The full day trip gives you ample time to check out the Manele Bay Resort before walking over to the harbor. You'll have time for a drink or meal and a walk around this lovely hotel. A car is definitely not necessary if you simply want to snorkel or swim.

Send off the hopelessly restless among you on a whirlwind car tour (try the Munro Trail north of Lana'i City if you have a jeep and it hasn't just rained) and some snorkeling in one day – providing you're on the first ferry of the day. Bring a picnic lunch, try the local fare in Lana'i City or splurge at the big resorts – both resorts have food the critics rave about. You can't see everything in one day, but you can have a great time and will want to return.

Lana'i has a shortage of water, and so makes good use of reclaimed water for both golf courses and landscaping; often even showers. Be aware that you shouldn't drink shower water. All beaches with any facilities will provide drinking water as well – sometimes in large coolers spread along the beach. Excursions bring their own water and other drinks, and paper cups as well. With all the sun, you'll need plenty of fluids, especially if you're soaking up the sun on the ship while in transit.

112

If you love the reef...

• Show respect for the reef creatures by causing them no harm.

• Do not touch the coral, for that damages it.

• Come as a respectful visitor, rather than as a predator.

• Leave the many beautiful creatures you find there in peace, so that others may enjoy them as you have.

• Think of the creatures of the reef as fellow travelers in our life journey, and then you may comprehend their magnificence.

SADDLEBACK BUTTERFLYFISH

MANELE HARBOR

This appears at first glance to be an unlikely-looking place to snorkel. However, it has an excellent assortment of fish and coral for such a small site. Simply step off the boat or ferry, snorkel in the little cove between the breakwater and the shore (completely protected from boat traffic). When calm, you can continue out to the right toward the point.

There's a grassy park next to the harbor with restrooms, indoor showers, drinking water, picnic tables and shade – everything except a beach. You could have a day trip right here. This is worth more than one snorkel and you'll probably have the little cove to yourself. Explore along the breakwater, and weave in and out among the coral heads towards the point.

GETTING THERE   *From the dock, turn left toward the little cove on the other side of the small breakwater. There's no beach, and entry is from the rocks at the left corner of the cove. See the map. Wear shoes even though it's a short distance because the rocks can be slippery, sharp, and sometimes hot. Entry is easy as long as you're careful not to slip. You'll wonder why you're here, until you duck your head underwater.* (see map, page 115).

HULOPO'E BAY

This large, beautiful bay in front of the Manele Bay Resort is quite famous, and for good reasons. The lovely wide sand beach has showers, restrooms, drinking water, grass, and shade. Limited camping is allowed here, with a permit that must be obtained in Maui. This is undoubtedly one of the finest beachside camping sites in all the islands.

When calm, you can snorkel anywhere, but don't miss the row of coral peninsulas jutting out like underwater ship piers over on the left all the way to the point. Cruise up the dramatic mini-canyons between them. We have seen spiny lobster here in the daytime, as well as pelagic fish, parrotfish, raccoon butterflyfish, boxfish, many wrasses, eels, and pods of spinner dolphins.

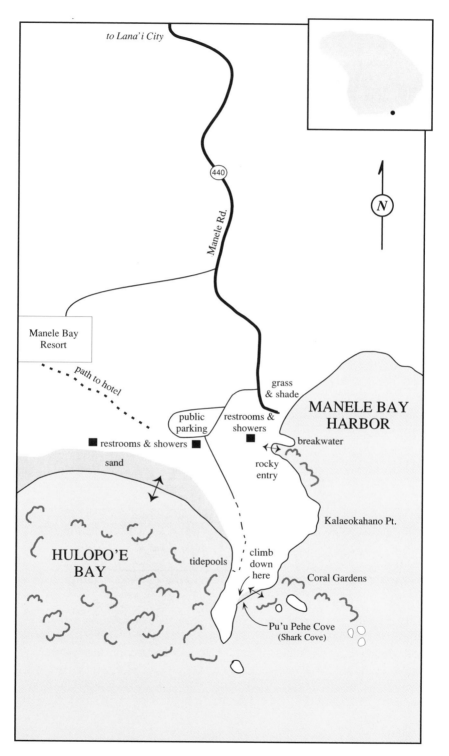

to Lana'i City

440

Manele Rd.

N

Manele Bay
Resort

path to hotel

grass
& shade

MANELE BAY
HARBOR

public
parking

restrooms &
showers

■ restrooms & showers ■   ■

breakwater

rocky
entry

sand

Kalaeokahano Pt.

HULOPO'E
BAY

tidepools

climb
down
here

Coral Gardens

Pu'u Pehe Cove
(Shark Cove)

115

If surf is high, don't get caught between the waves and coral or rocks. We saw a variety of weather in a few days – from calm as glass throughout the bay to breakers. Keep in mind that all of the Lana'i snorkeling sites face open ocean, so conditions vary depending on which way the waves are rolling.

Even if swell is breaking, good swimmers can usually go beyond, since the coral extends far out. Just don't go beyond the point if there's any current at all. The water is usually wonderfully clear. A good part of the bay is about 10-20' deep. On the far left you'll see stairs coming down from the hill to tidepools, which are fun for kids. Check the tide and surf conditions carefully first.

GETTING THERE *From the Manele Bay Hotel, follow the path down to the beach and continue to the far left for the best snorkeling.* (see map, page 115). *From the Manele Harbor it's a five to ten minute walk. Head out the exit road, and take the first left.*

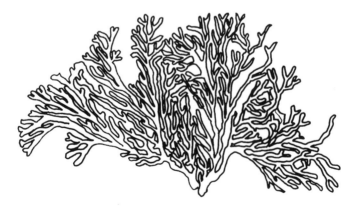

PU'U PEHE COVE

Pu'u Pehe Cove is also called Shark Cove. If you don't mind climbing down a very steep 20-30' cliff, which does have a crude trail, and is actually much easier than it looks, this bay has a pretty sandy beach and excellent snorkeling. No crowds down on this beach! Perhaps our favorite shore-entry site to snorkel on Lana'i.

Entry is easy from the sandy beach when calm. Snorkel to the left, continue as far as you like, unless you encounter currents near the far point. As always, waves can vary in size and come from different directions, so conditions are quite changeable from day to day. Since this beach is fairly isolated in spite of being so close to a big hotel, don't snorkel until you feel sure that you can easily handle the ocean conditions. Of course, never snorkel alone at a place like this.

GETTING THERE   *From Hulopo'e Bay, walk out on the dirt road toward the far left point, past the stairs to the tidepools* (see map, page 115). *Be sure to wear tennis shoes or reef shoes, hat and sunglasses (there's no shade). At the point we've marked on the map you'll find the only place to climb down the cliff on the far side. It can help if one person goes down first and another hands the gear down. It's not as difficult as it looks, providing you go slowly and hold on carefully. There are no facilities here and little shade, but it's dramatic and worthwhile.*

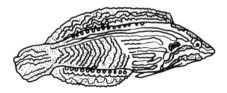

ELEGANT CORIS

KAUMALAPA'U HARBOR

Kaumalapa'u Harbor (often called Barge Harbor) is another unlikely-looking snorkeling site. It has fine snorkeling, however, and offers some unusual fish including pyramid butterflyfish. Don't go on a Thursday – the only day this big harbor is in full operation.

You'll find a small reef with fairly easy entry, clear water and lots to see. You do need to enter from rocks, slowly and carefully. Parking is no problem. Crowds are certainly no problem. Small waves break over the shallow reef in the center, making it look rougher than it really is. Swimming around the outside of the reef was easy and quite safe, but I would hesitate to swim directly over such a shallow reef. Experts can manage it when the tide is right.

GETTING THERE   *From Lana'i City, take Highway 440 west to the harbor. Since Lana'i doesn't have many roads, it's easy to find* (see map, page 108). *Use the harbor parking lot and snorkel on the right side where you can see the reef from the lot* (see map, page 119). *It's right next to shore. Enter to the left of the reef from the rocks and swim entirely around it if you wish.*

SHARK FIN ROCK

This is a spacious snorkel and dive location, which can only be reached by boat (assuming you didn't bring your own helicopter), since it's surrounded by high cliffs. A very dramatic location, this site derives its name from a large rock in the shape of a shark's fin. There are numerous little coves to explore for as far you can swim. The coral isn't spectacular here, but plenty of fish hang out near the rocks. Mostly about 10-20' deep near shore. Divers can head to deeper water.

Shark Fin and Cathedrals sites are located on the southern shore of Lana'i. Trilogy runs a small catamaran as an optional daytrip for their Lana'i excursion clients, and it's delightful. Scuba is offered here as well. You may find other excursions from Maui that visit here. A shelf of coral extends out from the cliffs at just the right height for snorkelers. You will probably be the only group of snorkelers in sight if you come here. Of course, if you are feeling brave and indestructible, you could jump in from the high cliffs as ancient Hawai'ians did. Getting out would be another matter!

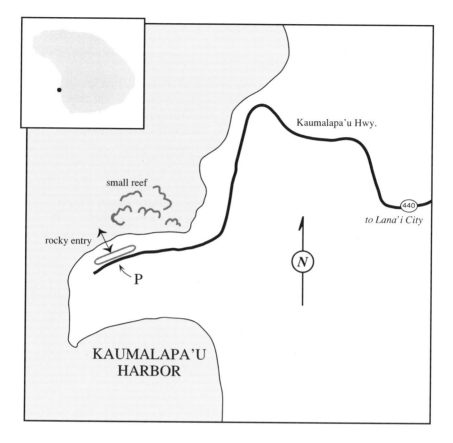

small reef

rocky entry

P

Kaumalapa'u Hwy.

440

to Lana'i City

N

KAUMALAPA'U HARBOR

SEA STAR

MARINE LIFE

The coral reef supports tremendous diversity in a small space. On a healthy reef, you've never seen everything, because of the boggling variety of species, as well as changes from day to day and changes from day to night. The reef functions much like the oasis in the desert providing food (more abundant than the open ocean) and shelter from predators. Only the wild rainforests can compare with the reef in complexity.

In Hawai'i the reef coral itself is less spectacular than in warmer waters of the world. This is counterbalanced by the colorful and abundant fish, which provide quite a show.

There are excellent color fish identification cards available in bookstores and dive shops. We particularly like the ones published by Natural World Press. There are also many good marine life books that give far more detailed descriptions of each creature than we attempt in these brief notes.

FISH NOTES

OCTOPUS

Some varieties of octopuses hide during the day, but others will hunt for food then. They eat shrimp, fish, crabs, and mollusks – you should eat so well! Octopuses have strong "beaks" and can bite humans, so it's safer to not handle them, especially those that have a poisonous bite to stun their prey.

Being mollusks without shells, they must rely on speed, cunning and camouflage to escape danger. Octopuses are capable of imitating a flashing sign, or changing their color and texture to match their surroundings in an instant. This makes them very hard to spot, even when they're hiding in plain sight – usually on the bottom or on rocks. They can also squirt an ink to confuse predators or prey. Special "nozzles" can squirt water shooting them around quickly. They live about two years.

REEF SQUID

These graceful, iridescent creatures hang around reef areas, often forming a single long line. All eyes will follow you easily since they have 360 degree vision. They can capture surprisingly large fish with their tentacles.

SHRIMP

In all kinds, colors, and sizes, they like to hide in rocks and coral – often living symbiotically with the coral. They are difficult to spot during the daytime, but at night you will notice lots of tiny pairs of eyes reflected in the flashlight glare. Most are fairly small and well disguised.

Some examples include: the harlequin shrimp (brightly colored) that eat sea stars, the banded coral shrimp (found all over the world), and numerous tiny shrimp that you won't see without magnification.

SEA URCHINS

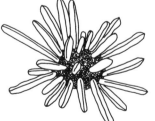

Concealed tube feet allow urchins to move around in their hunt for algae. The collector urchin has pebbles and bits of coral attached for camouflage. Collector urchins are quite common in Hawai'i, and have no spines.

Beware of purple-black urchins with long spines. These are common in shallow water at certain beaches. It's not the long spines that get you, it's the ones beneath. The bright red pencil sea urchin is common and easy to spot. Although large, its spines aren't sharp enough to be a problem for people.

CRINOIDS

These animals seen on top of the rocks or coral can easily be mistaken for plants. They are sometimes called "feather stars" and are delicate and beautiful plankton feeders.

SEA STARS

Abundant, in many colors and styles. The crown of thorns sea star, which can be such a devastator of coral reefs, is found in Hawai'i, but not in large numbers like the South Pacific. Sea stars firmly grasp their prey with strong suction cups, and then eat at leisure.

RAYS

Manta rays (unusually large for plankton-eaters) use two flaps to guide plankton into their huge efficient mouths. Mantas often grow to be two meters from wing-tip to wing-tip, and can weigh 300 pounds. Even larger specimens are sometimes seen by divers. They can't sting, but are large enough to bump hard.

Mantas feed at night by doing forward rolls in the water with mouths wide open. Lights will attract plankton which appeal to the manta rays. Dive boats in certain locations can easily attract them with their bright lights making the night trips quite exciting.

Another beautiful ray, the spotted eagle ray, is less common, but can sometimes be seen cruising the bottom for food and can grow to be seven feet across. They have a dark back with lots of small white dots and an extremely long tail. Their fins function more like wings to enable them to "fly" along rather than swimming. Common sting rays prefer the sandy bottom and stay in calm, shallow, warmer water.

EELS

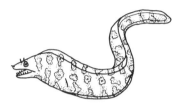

Moray eels abound among the reefs of Maui. They can easily grow up to two meters long.

Varieties of moray found in Hawai'i include whitemouth, snowflake, zebra (black and white stripes), wavy-lined, mottled, and dragon moray (often reddish-brown with distinct white spots of differing sizes).

Morays prefer to hide in holes during the day. If out cruising, they will find a nearby hole when spotting a snorkeler. When they stick out their heads and breathe, their teeth are most impressive.

Eels generally have no interest in eating snorkelers, other than very annoying ones, while they would be quite happy and able to swallow a fairly large fish.

TRUMPETFISH

These long, skinny fish can change color, often bright yellow or light blue – and will change right in front of your eyes. They sometimes hang upright to blend with their environment, lying in wait to suck in their prey. Sometimes they "shadow" another fish to sneak up on prey – even at a cleaning station.

They do eat during the day, which is unusual for fish-eaters, who usually eat at dawn or dusk. Trumpetfish are quite common in Hawai'i and often seen alone. Some grow to more than one meter long.

NEEDLEFISH

These pointed, common silvery-blue fish like swimming very near the surface, usually in schools – sometimes leaping from the water. Needlefish are as long and skinny as their name implies, and grow to as much as 1-2' long. Color and markings vary, but the long narrow shape is distinctive and hard to mistake. They're usually bluish on top, and translucent below for camouflage.

BUTTERFLYFISH

Butterflyfish are beautiful, colorful, abundant and varied in Hawai'i. They have incredible coloration, typically bright yellow, white, orange and black, with a little blue. They hang out near coral, eating algae, sponges, tube worms and coral polyps. No one really understands the purpose of their beautiful colors, but many have speculated. Perhaps they serve territorial needs.

Juveniles are often distinctly different in coloring. Bizarre patterns may confuse predators – especially since they can pivot fast. Bars may help some hide, while stripes are seen more in faster fish. Black lines across the eyes and spots near the tail also provide camouflage.

Butterflyfish are often seen in pairs remaining together for up to three years. They're delightful to watch, fast and fascinating. Hovering and turning are more important to them than speed since they stay near shelter of the reef and catch a quick meal – like a tube worm.

The ones you are most likely to see in Hawai'i include: raccoon (reminding you of the face of the animal), ornate (with bright orange lines making it easy to spot), threadfin (another large, beautiful one), saddleback, lemon (very tiny), bluestripe (a beautiful one found only in Hawai'i), fourspot, milletseed, oval, teardrop, and forceps (also called long nose).

An interesting one is the pyramid, which can darken its white body, then light up a spot in the center, making it look just as though it swallowed a light bulb. The lined butterflyfish is the largest variety found in Hawai'i.

Many butterflyfish have black spots near the tail – perhaps to confuse a predator about which way they're headed.

PARROTFISH

Among the most dramatically colored fish on the reef, male parrotfish are blue, green, turquoise, yellow, lavender, and/or orange with assorted variations of these colors. Females tend to be reddish brown. No two are alike. Parrotfish are very beautiful, with artistic, abstract markings.

These fish change colors at different times in their lives and can also change sex as needed. They can be quite large (up to 1 1/2 meters).

Patient grazers, they spend countless hours scraping algae from dead coral with their large, beak-like teeth, and create tons of white sand in the process. Most prefer to zoom away from snorkelers, but you'll see them passing gracefully by.

125

TRIGGERFISH

Fond of sea urchins as a main course, triggerfish graze during the day on algae, worms and other small items.

Varieties include the Picasso (wildly colorful – not too many at each beach, but worth watching for), reef (the Hawai'ian state fish), pinktail (easy to identify with its black body, white fins and pink tail), black (common, distinctive white lines between body and fins). The checkerboard triggerfish has a pink tail, yellow-edged fins, and blue stripes on its face. All triggerfish are very beautiful and fascinating to watch.

FILEFISH

The scrawled filefish has blue scribbles and brown dots over its olive green body. Quite large, up to one meter, often in pairs, but seen occasionally in groups.

A filefish will often turn its body flat to your view, and raise its top spine in order to impress you. This lets you have a great close-up view.

The brown filefish (endemic) is much smaller, with lines on its head and white spots on its brown body. The fantail filefish (also endemic and small) has a distinct orange tail and lots of black spots over a light body. Filefish will sometimes change color patterns rapidly for camouflage.

SURGEONFISH

Razor-sharp fin-like spines on each side of the tail are the hallmark of this fish, quite common in Hawai'i. These spines provide excellent defense, but aren't needed to fend off tourists since surgeonfish can easily swim away.

Varieties includes the orangeband surgeonfish (with distinctive long, bright orange marks on the side), as well as the Achilles tang (also called naso tang), which has bright orange spots surrounding the spines near the orange tail. The yellow tang is completely yellow and smaller. The sailfin tang has dramatic vertical markings. It's less common, but easy to identify.

WRASSES

Wrasses are amazingly bright and multicolored fish. Some very small ones set themselves up for business and operate a cleaning station, where they clean much larger fish without having to worry about becoming dinner. They eat parasites, and provide an improbable reef service in the process. Perhaps their bright colors serve as "neon" signs to advertise their services.

In Hawai'i, the cleaner wrasse is bright yellow, purple and black. Other wrasses are large including the dazzling yellowtail (up to 15"), which has a red body covered with glowing blue spots, a few stripes, and a bright yellow tail.

Another large wrasse, the saddleback, is endemic to Hawai'i. It is bright blue, with green and orange markings. Wrasses are closely related to parrotfish. Like parrotfish, they can change colors and sex.

SCORPIONFISH

This improbable-looking fish is very colorful, with feather-like multicolor spines. Beware of their poisonous spines, though! Don't even think about touching a scorpionfish, and try to avoid accidentally stepping on one.

This varied group of exotic fish includes the bright red Hawai'ian turkeyfish, sometimes called a lionfish.

Others are so well-camouflaged that they are hard to see. They just lurk on the bottom blending in well with the sand and coral. If you see one, count yourself lucky.

PUFFERFISH

Pufferfish (and the related trunkfish) swim slowly, so need more protection. Some can blow up like balloons when threatened.

Two kinds are common in sheltered areas: porcupine (displaying spines when inflated), and spotted trunkfish and boxfish (typically brown or black with lots of white dots). They tend to prefer to escape under the coral, although some seem unafraid of snorkelers.

SHARKS

Although sharks have quite a reputation for teeth rather than brains, they are unquestionably survivors, having been around for about 300 million years.

This is an extremely successful species with keen hearing, smell, sight and ability to detect electrical signals through the water. They swim with a side-to-side motion, which does not make them speedy by ocean standards. When snorkeling you are unlikely to spot any shark except the reef or white-tipped lazing around shallow water. Plenty of larger species pass by Hawai'i, but tend to prefer the deeper waters in the channels.

WHALES

Humpback whales migrate here to breed in winter, around mid-December. Humpbacks come quite close to the coast, where you can watch whole families. They are so large that you can often easily see them spouting and breaching. If you bring binoculars, you can see them well from shore. Their great size never fails to impress, as does their fluid, seemingly effortless graceful movement in the water.

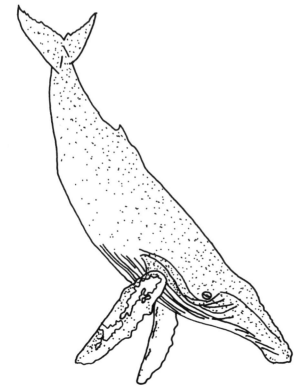

DOLPHINS

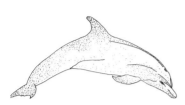

Spinner dolphins are frequently seen in large schools. They swim as small family groups within these schools, and often swim fast, leaping from the water, spinning in the air. They tend to hang out in certain locations, so you can search them out if you like.

Bottlenose dolphins often approach fast-moving boats, and it is a great thrill to watch them race along just next to the bow of your boat, jumping in and out of the water with grace and easy speed. Beaked dolphins are also commonly seen in Hawai'i.

SEA TURTLES

Common at many Maui reefs, though they usually stay away from humans. Some do seem nearly tame – or at least unconcerned about snorkelers.

Sea turtles are often seen in pairs. Larger specimens (often seen at Maluaka and Five Graves) might be more than 100 years old, and tend to be docile and unafraid. You'll often see them resting on the bottom in about ten to twenty feet of water during the day. They will let you swim as close as you like, but if you hover over them, they might be afraid to come up for air.

Do not disturb these graceful creatures, so that they can remain unafraid to swim among snorkelers. In Hawai'i it is against the law to touch or harass these magnificent animals.

WEATHER

All islands have a windward side, which is wetter, and a leeward side which is drier. In Hawai'i, the northeast is windward and hence wet, and the southwest is leeward, or kona, and hence drier and sunnier. Waves from afar tend to arrive from the north in winter and from the south in summer, although this pattern can change often.

Hawai'i gets most of its rain in the winter. The most severe storms ("kona"), however, come from the south and can even bring hurricanes in the summer. Temperatures tend to be very mild year-round, yet there is variety any day of the year. There are days when you could tan in Kihei in the morning, drive up to cold Haleakala later, while rain continues in Hana. Generally summer temperatures are at least five degrees F warmer than winter.

Evaporating moisture from the ocean forms clouds. As the clouds rise over the mountains, they cool, and the condensing moisture becomes rain. The West Maui Mountains receive 400" of rain a year, while nearby Lahaina only gets about 30".

Having lost most of their moisture in passing over the mountains, the clouds have little left for the leeward side – so it is in the rain shadow of the mountains. The leeward weather is therefore often sunny. Waikiki, Poipu, Ka'anapali, and Kona are all rain shadowed. On Maui if you get stuck in heavy rains in Hana, just head for Kihei or Wailua to find the sun.

Changeable is the word for Maui's weather – not just between areas, but also rapidly changeable in any given place. The trade winds blow about 90% of the time in the summer and about 50% in the winter. They tend to be stronger in the afternoon.

The following weather notes focus on the leeward or west coasts, since that is where most tourists are heading. The windward or eastern coasts have much more rain, wind and waves.

SEASONAL CHANGES

Maui has much milder weather than the continental United States. Yet it is has seasons you might call winter, spring and summer. At 20°N Latitude, there are nearly 2 1/2 hours more sun in midsummer than in midwinter, which is 21% more. But the moderating effect of the ocean keeps temperature swings quite moderate.

Winter is the cooler, wetter season. Cooler is a relative term, as the average high temperature in winter falls to a brisk 80° F, as opposed to a summer average high of 88° F. Water temperature in winter falls to around 77° F, and at times, wind, rain and cooler air temperatures can temper your desire to splash around in the water. Winter usually begins in mid-November, with the start of winter storms from the north-northwest. This is the start of the large wave season on the north coast. Winter tails off in mid-March.

Spring really is just the transition from winter to summer, and is marked by the end of winter storms in mid-March. Hours of sunshine go up, especially on the west, leeward side of the island. This can be a very pleasant time of year. Spring transitions into summer in May.

Summer begins in May, as the weather warms, and the rains slacken. Tradewinds temper the heat and humidity almost all the time. This is prime sunning and play time. An occasional tropical storm or hurricane can come through, and swells can roll in from the South. The heat softens in October as summer draws to an end.

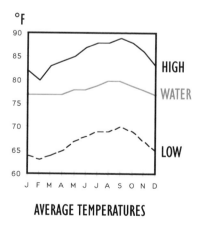

AVERAGE TEMPERATURES

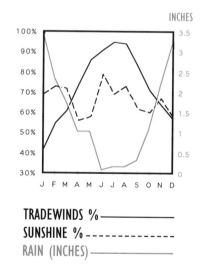

TRADEWINDS % ————————
SUNSHINE % - - - - - - - - - - - - -
RAIN (INCHES) ————————

JANUARY: This month offers an opportunity for the wettest weather all year. It's also one of the coolest. Large surf can often pound the north and west exposed beaches.

FEBRUARY: Just as cool, the surf continues to hit the north and west exposed beaches, although storms are a bit less frequent.

MARCH: The weather starts to improve with fewer storms, especially on West Maui.

APRIL: Spring arrives early, so warm weather begins during this month.

MAY: Summer is already arriving – especially in Western Maui. This tends to be a trouble-free month.

JUNE: This offers very warm and dry weather with plenty of sun. Fortunately the winds blow nearly every day.

JULY: Much the same as June, except that storms in the South Pacific begin at this time. They hit beaches exposed to the south.

AUGUST: Another warm month, occasional big waves can hit the southern exposed beaches.

SEPTEMBER: This last month of summer can sometimes be the hottest and most humid. Hurricanes rarely strike Maui and Lana'i, but they are most common this month. They usually miss the islands, but bring muggy weather.

OCTOBER: Milder weather begins this month with the start of storms arriving from the north.

NOVEMBER: Sometimes the first real winter storms arrive and they can be somewhat cool.

DECEMBER: This is winter with frequent storms and wind bringing big waves to the exposed northern and western beaches. However, even this month can be clear and warm between storms.

Coolest month:	February
Hottest month:	September
Rainiest month:	January
Driest month:	June
Coolest water:	December-April
Warmest water:	August-September

134

TIDES

Tides are very slight in Maui, with the average difference between high and low only 2'- 3' max. It's a good idea to know which way the tide is going because tidal flow does affect the currents. If the tide is going out, you might want to avoid snorkeling in places where water is already shallow or currents tend to sweep out of a bay, often the center, or a gap in the reef (*see Understanding waves, page 33*). For most of Maui's beaches, this has very little effect.

WATER TEMPERATURE

On the surface the water in Maui averages a low of about 77° F (25° C) in March to a high of about 80° F (27° C) in September. Sheltered bays can be a bit warmer, while deeper or rough water can be surprisingly cool. Kaua'i (further north) can be even cooler. If you happen to be slender, no longer young, or from a moderate climate, this can seem cooler than you might like – especially if you like to snorkel for hours.

HURRICANES

Summer is hurricane season, but it is also the time when weather is usually excellent. The storms don't last long, but can be terribly destructive. Hurricanes can bring amazingly heavy rain and winds to all the islands. Any of the islands could receive a direct hit. Maui has escaped major damage from hurricanes in recent years.

TSUNAMIS

Huge waves can be triggered by earthquakes either locally or far across the Pacific. They've hit Hawai'i numerous times, more often from the north. Some very destructive tsunamis have hit and swept over the lowest land. Depending on the exact direction, they can directly hit a valley and really wipe it out and rinse it clean. It is probably better to not be there when this happens, unless you're one great surfer dude.

Currently there's plenty of warning and authorities prefer to warn of every possible tsunami just to be safe. It doesn't pay to ignore warnings just because the sea appears calm. If a major earthquake strikes while you're visiting, it's a good idea to head rapidly for high ground. Leave bays or valleys which can act to funnel the effects of a large wave.

GEOLOGY

To understand what's happening today in Hawai'i, begin by casting your thoughts back to about 30 million years ago. At that time lava was bubbling out in the middle of the Pacific about 20,000' below the ocean surface, due to a volcanic hot spot directly underneath. Molten rock pushing up through the ocean floor formed volcanoes under the sea. Lava built up, layer after layer until it finally reached the surface to form the first island.

As the volcanoes grew, the weight of these early islands gradually caused them to sink down again, forming atolls. The Pacific Plate drifted northwest, while the hot spot remained stationary. A long string of more than 30 islands were formed, stretching from Midway Island southeast 1600 miles all the way to the Big Island. Another island is already rising in the sea close to the southeast side of the Big Island. Loihi Sea Mount is now just 3000' under the surface, and will probably join the Big Island as it emerges. Lava flowing into the sea from Kilauea has been intermittently building the Big Island daily toward Loihi.

Most of the current above-water mass is now concentrated in eight islands. Kaua'i, about 5 million years old, is the oldest of these, while the Big Island is less than 1 million years old. As these islands drift around 4" northwest each year, the lava conduits to their volcanoes bend until new conduits are formed. Eventually, the next volcano in the chain takes over the job of releasing the unremitting pressure from pools of magma far below. The beautiful Haleakala Crater on Maui is now considered extinct and offers a chance to explore one of the Hawai'ian volcanoes.

AND A LITTLE NATURAL HISTORY, TOO

When each underground mountain emerges from the sea, coral larvae begin to establish their new homes on the volcanic rocks around the base. Stony coral is one of the first ocean creatures to reach and become established on a new island.

These larvae travel island by island – originally coming in a very round-about fashion on the currents from the ancient reefs surrounding Indonesia. Once they became established, it was easier for new larvae to reach the next nearby island. The reef begins as a fringe around the island. Each polyp of coral secretes a skeleton of calcium carbonate. Gradually the colony grows large enough to provide a home for other plants and animals.

All of the major Hawai'ian islands now have fringing reefs around much of the shore. The Big Island, still in formation, is not yet fully surrounded by reef. As the islands grow, get heavy and gradually sink, the reef changes as well. The older islands of Kaua'i and O'ahu have very old coral reef deposits on land – remnants of a time when the sea level was higher.

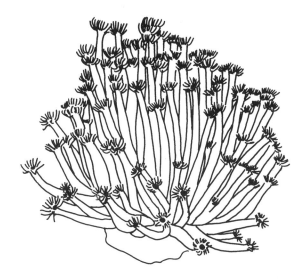

Coral reefs are made up of coral animals and algae growing on top of the dead skeletons of former creatures. In search of sunlight, they continue to grow upward toward the light, as they need to stay within 150' of the surface of the sea.

The outside of a reef grows faster than the inner surface, so eventually a lagoon forms between the reef and the land. The reef is then called a barrier reef, limited examples of which can be found at places in Kaua'i and O'ahu.

Since the currents in Hawai'i come mainly from Japan rather than the warmer south Pacific, they bring less variety of sea life. Larvae need to survive long enough to reach an island and establish themselves before sending out the next generation, so it's helpful to have stepping-stone islands in order to have greater variety. Most will not survive long enough to cross the large open Pacific ocean.

Tahiti, for example, has a much greater variety of coral because of the stepping-stone islands leading all the way from Southeast Asia. Hawai'i, in contrast, is one of the most isolated island groups in the world. It also has somewhat cooler water and less sunlight than Tahiti, making it less hospitable to some species. This isolation has kept all species of plant and animal life rather limited, and also encouraged the evolution of unique species found only in Hawai'i. These unique species are referred to as "endemic". They give Hawai'i a special character – both above and below the water. More than 30% of the fish seen here are found nowhere else in the world.

For millions of years the Hawai'ian Islands had no plants or animals in spite of the rich soil, due to their 2000 mile isolation from other large land masses. When plants and animals finally did arrive, they had little competition and a superb climate. The lack of competition meant plants did not require thorns or other protective features. Some plants and animals found such a perfect environment that they thrived. Before man arrived, Hawai'i had no fruits or vegetables. The Polynesians, and later Europeans, changed this environment enormously by their imports and cultivation.

Most of the "exotic" plants that you may think of as quintessentially Hawai'ian were brought by man (mango, papaya, pineapple, orchid, ginger, hibiscus). Koa and ohia (the Hawai'ian state tree), on the other hand, pre-date man's arrival. Ohia is often the first to grow on lava flows and has produced much of the Hawai'ian rain forest.

Unfortunately, most of the rain forest has already been destroyed by animals brought by man (such as cattle and goats) or cleared to provide land for sugar production. Sugar and pineapple production now appear to be on the way out, a casualty of world economics. Tourism has now replaced these crops, but takes its own toll on the fragile islands of Hawai'i.

REEF DEVELOPMENT

Hawai'ian reefs have weathered at least four major changes in the distant past. Many land-based plants and animals also became extinct during these changes and others took their place. Current reefs are composed mostly of shallow water reef coral. They incorporate algae in their structure, and the algae is dependent on photosynthesis.

Different plants and animals live in the varied locations on the reef depending primarily on wave action. Species living on the outer edge of the reef are skilled at surviving strong waves and currents. Lagoon species don't have to endure this, so the lagoon supports more delicate life as well.

Hawai'i has a number of strikingly different reef habitats – each with its own story to tell. Where the water is rough, cauliflower coral dominates. The more delicate finger coral grows only in the calm lagoon areas. Large boulders are common in the open waters, especially where wave action is heaviest, and they support entirely different creatures. Caves, caverns and old lava tubes are quite abundant here. Steep drop-offs (like the back of Molokini Island) serve as an upwelling source of plankton-rich water, which attracts many larger creatures to feed. Sandy habitat is found in abundance on Maui. A thriving reef is developing around much of the island.

SPONGES

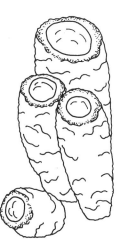

HISTORY

The islands of Hawai'i sat in dramatic isolation for millions of years, slowly softening their volcanic profile, while developing a soft green backdrop. The first people to arrive in the islands were from Polynesia, a culture with a long history of island hopping, dating back to their migration to Polynesia from the Middle East in large double hulled boats.

Fiji was settled by about 3500 B.C., then Samoa and Tonga, and later Tahiti. Hawai'i itself was first settled in waves beginning at least 1200 years ago, probably by voyagers from Tahiti and the Marquesas. They brought everything they needed for a new life here: chickens, dogs, pigs, coconut, bananas. The first landing may have been on the Kona Coast. Many were apparently looking for a form of religious freedom and prospered in this new land. To migrate this far over open ocean required considerable planning and navigational skill, as well as strong motivation.

PETROGLYPH

MAUI

Maui was formed by two volcanoes attached by a low section of land in the center – giving it the nickname "The Valley Island." The oldest volcano, Mauna Kahalawai, created the western section of Maui. Later Haleakala created the eastern part, leaving a huge and fascinating crater, which is now dormant.

Maui remained relatively independent until Chief Kahekili took over Lana'i and Moloka'i – the closest islands. Soon King Kamehameha I from the Big Island forcefully took over Maui as well as most of the other Hawai'ian islands and established his capital in Lahaina. Kamehameha II ruled from 1819 to 1824, but was much weaker and left decisions to Ka'ahumanu (Kamehameha I's favorite wife, who happened to be born in Hana). This was a period of transition away from traditional ways leaving the path clear just as the missionaries and whalers started to arrive. The resulting culture clash was chaos for the Hawai'ians. Although the Kamehameha dynasty was to last 88 years, the times were in flux. The monarchy was over when Queen Lili'uokalani was imprisoned in her own palace – opening Hawai'i to the big business interests. The growers soon arrived with their plantation system and imported laborers (mostly from Japan, China, and the Philipines). They saw profits from fields of sugar cane and pineapple, neither viable crops for Hawai'i these days. Macadamian nuts, sweet onions, coffee, wine, and marijuana have gradually taken the place of the older crops.

Maui has attracted very large numbers of tourists (with over two millions visitors each year) complete with huge hotels, miles of condos, golf courses, competing ships to take you on excursions, and plenty of restaurants, shopping and art galleries. This is quite an industry for an island of little more than 100,000 population.

LANA'I

Lana'i remained unsettled long after the Polynesians arrived on the other Hawai'ian islands, due to its relatively arid climate. Even today the population (2,800) remains quite small for its size. The Mormon Church bought large sections of the island in 1863, hoping to develop a community here. This never happened and title managed to stay with Mr Gibson, who had made the purchase for them.

In 1917 Mr Baldwin purchased most of the island. He sold it for a profit to the Dole Pineapple Company in 1922. Dole proceeded to build a company town to house the workers, many brought from the Philipines – creating the present Lana'i City. Castle and Cooke still owns most of this island and is experimenting with alternative crops, but none on a large scale at this time leaving most of the island untouched. At one time Lana'i was covered with pineapples, and even known as the Pineapple Island, but these days are gone. Pineapple productions is no longer economic here, since they can be produced cheaper in the South Pacific and elsewhere. Now only about 150 acres of pineapple remain for local consumption.

Lana'i is about 98% privately owned. It is legally part of the county that includes Maui and Moloka'i. These three islands would be one if the sea were lower. The other two islands with their high mountains block much of the rain before it reaches Lana'i, so this island doesn't receive enough rainfall on most of the island to support agriculture without irrigation.

Tourism appears to be a better source of income for the present. Manele Bay Resort (with its delightful location overlooking Hulopo'e Bay) and The Lodge at Koele (set in the midst of Norfolk Pines up in the hills) are attracting upscale travellers looking for superb accommodations in a serene setting. Each has its own spectacular golf course, which relies on recycled water.

LANGUAGE

English is now the official language of the islands of Hawai'i –
except for the island of Ni'ihau. However, most place names and lots
of slang are Hawai'ian, so it's most helpful to at least be able to
pronounce Hawai'ian enough to be understood. It's a very straight-
forward phonetic language – each letter is usually pronounced just
one way. The long place names aren't nearly so daunting when
you've learned the system.

All syllables begin with a consonant that is followed by at least one
vowel. When the missionaries attempted to write this spoken
language, they used only seven consonants (h,k,l,m,n,p,w) and five
vowels (a,e,i,o,u). More recently, in an effort to help outsiders
pronounce Hawai'ian, the glottal stop has been added – marked by '.
For example, in *Hawai'i*, the ' is used to indicate that each *i* should
be pronounced separately: Ha-wai-i, rather than Ha-waii.

A horizontal line called a macron is often placed over vowels to be
given a longer duration. Technically, each and every letter is
pronounced in Hawai'ian, except for a few vowel combinations.
However, locals often shorten names a bit, so listen carefully to the
way natives pronounce a name. Another addition to the language is a
form of pidgin, which served to ease the difficulties of having
multiple languages spoken. Laborers were brought in speaking
Japanese, Mandarin, Cantonese, Portuguese, English, as well as
other languages, and they had to be able to work together. Pidgin
evolved as an ad hoc, but surprisingly effective way to communicate,
and much of it survives in slang and common usage today.

PRONUNCIATION

Consonants are pronounced the same as in English, except that the
W sometimes sounds more like a V when it appears in the middle
of a word. Vowels are pronounced as follows:

a = long as in father
e = short as in den, or long as the *ay* in say
i = long as the *ee* in see
o = round as in no
u = round as the *ou* in you

When vowels are joined (as they often are), pronounce each, with
slightly more emphasis on the first one. This varies with local usage.

142

a'a = rough lava (of Hawai'ian origin, now used worldwide)
ahi = yellowfin tuna (albacore)
ahupua'a = land division in pie shape from mountain to sea
ali'i = chief
aloha = hello, goodbye, expressing affection, showing kindness
haole = foreigner (now usually meaning a white person)
heiau = temple, religious platform
hukilau = joining together to pull in the net, then have a party
hula = native Hawai'ian dance
humuhumunukunukuapua'a = trigger fish that is Hawai'ian state fish
imu = pit for steaming food over hot stones
kahuna = powerful priest
kai = sea
kama'aina = long-time resident of the islands
kaola = barbequed
kapu = taboo
kaukau = food
kona = leeward, or away from the direction of the wind
kukui = candlenut (state tree)
lei = garland of flowers, shells, etc. given as a symbol of affection
lu'au = Hawai'ian traditional feast, including roast pork and poi
mahalo = thanks; admiration, praise, respect
mahi mahi = dolphinfish (not a dolphin)
makai = on the seaside, towards the sea, or in that direction
malihini = recent arrival to the islands, tourist, stranger
mana = power coming from the spirit world
mano = shark
mauka = inland, upland, towards the mountains; in that direction
mauna = mountain, peak
menehune = little people of legend, here before the Polynesians
moana = ocean
nene = Hawai'ian state bird
niu = coconut
'ohana = extended family
'ono = the best, delicious, savory; to relish or crave
pa'hoehoe = lava that has a smooth texture
pakalolo = marijuana
pali = cliff
pu pu = appetizer
taro = starchy rootplant used to make poi
wahine = female
wai = fresh water
wana = black spined sea urchin

TRAVEL TIPS

GETTING THERE

Most flights arrive via Kahului Airport. Nearby rental cars can be reached by shuttle. The airport area is well-signed, with easy-to-find freeways heading in all directions. Large, busy gas stations are located just to the west. Plenty of shopping is available if you want to pick up supplies on your way to a condo. You'll see Costco on the left as you leave the airport area going west. The stream of arriving tourists is quite impressive, but the airport's efficiency makes it easy to get right to the beaches when arriving midday.

Kapalua West Maui Airport is much closer to the Kapalua-Ka'anapali area, avoiding the traffic across the island. However, few flights make use of this smaller airport.

It's possible to fly to Lana'i by way of Kahului, but it's usually easier and often faster or more convenient to fly by way of Honolulu or take the ferry from Lahaina to Lana'i. Schedules change frequently, so check on current connections.

TRAVEL LIGHT

Learn to travel light – experienced travelers know why and how:

- Traveling carry-on-only eliminates any risk and worry about lost or delayed luggage, which can wreak havoc on your vacation.

- Not having checked luggage makes it easy to catch an earlier connection – just walk on. It also gives you the opportunity to be voluntarily bumped for compensation – which happens often on these heavily booked flights.

- Traveling carry-on only forces you to pack lighter, which is easier on the back when you have to lug everything around.

- Because you don't have to check any bags, there's less standing in line required. It's typical to save an hour or more each way when you have no luggage to check in and out.

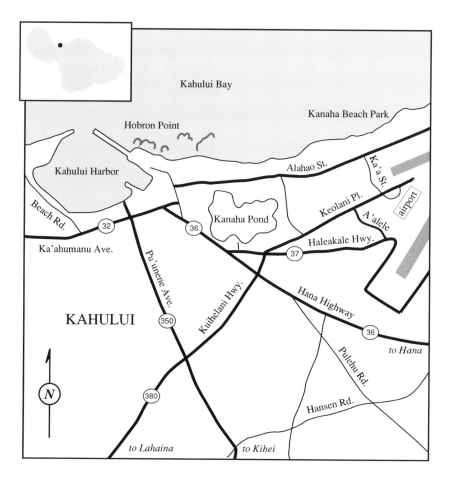

Kahului Bay

Kanaha Beach Park

Hobron Point

Kahului Harbor

Alahao St.

Ka'a St.

airport

Keolani Pl.

A'alele

Beach Rd.

32

Ka'ahumanu Ave.

36

Kanaha Pond

Haleakale Hwy.

37

KAHULUI

Pu'unene Ave.

Kuihelani Hwy.

350

Hana Highway

36

to Hana

N

380

Pulehu Rd.

Hansen Rd.

to Lahaina

to Kihei

LONGNOSE BUTTERFLYFISH

145

LEARNING TO PACK LIGHT

- Develop a wardrobe where everything goes with everything else. Pick a basic color you like – maybe khaki or denim, which won't show dirt so much – then add bright touches with shirts. Polo-type lightweight knit cotton short-sleeve shirts suit the climate well. Casual shirts are popular and easy to find, either in mainland styles, or floral styles developed here. Locals prefer a comfortable look. Even weddings and parties welcome people in either casual or more formal attire. It's a charming Hawai'ian tradition in tune with the tropics.

- Use layers. One sweater for the plane will also suffice for all cool circumstances in Hawai'i (unless camping or heading for high altitude). Only in the winter do you need to consider a second sweater or jacket.

- Sandals are acceptable everywhere and easily available at shops and markets. If you don't have any, get them once you arrive, as the variety is probably better than at home. Tennis shoes or hiking boots are necessary for hikes and lava, but this heavy stuff can be worn on the plane if it won't fit in your carry-on.

- Reef shoes and flip-flops are available everywhere, too; however, don't count on easily finding your size in exactly the style you like. Retailers don't necessarily get to choose their sizes, and can end up with lots of odd sizes and colors.

- Make yourself a simple cotton shoe bag, to help keep your bag clean, or use a plastic kitchen trash bag.

- Wear shorts everywhere if you want to blend in (except at very tony resort dining rooms). Even these have been known to make exceptions for paying guests. Long pants are the exception, unless you're working or in a formal situation.

- Use a packable hat, unless you prefer to wear one for the flight. A broad-brim lightweight hat is worth carrying on, if you have one you like.

- It's becoming popular to take a travel vest with lots of pockets for the plane and day trips. This can eliminate the need for a purse or bag, and makes it easy to carry whatever matters to you, such as sunscreen, snacks, folding hairbrush, medicine, reading glasses, a small pen, and so forth.

VALUABLES

Theft is mostly a problem with rental cars, tourist parking areas and popular beaches or remote beaches – a bit worse on O'ahu because of the larger population, but seen on all the popular islands these days. Of course, urban theft is becoming common in many mainland cities, so why should the Hawai'ian islands be an exception?

Don't get mad – get ready. Follow some easy and sensible precautions. You can greatly decrease your chances of having a problem and also minimize the impact on your vacation if you do get unlucky. Even with our extensive travel in Hawai'i (always with a rental car and often to remote locations) we have never had a single theft. We try not to make ourselves a juicy target, and that seems to help our odds.

It's probably more common to simply lose things – particularly keys. The following ideas are useful for travel to any destination – by no means limited to Hawai'i:

- Leave nothing valuable in your car, not even in the trunk. If what you leave is not valuable, make that obvious. You don't want someone to take your old clothes thinking a wallet might be included. It's best to leave the car unlocked, as a common report in the papers is 'smashed side window', which can cost you more than a theft! On a hot day, it's a luxury to be able to leave the windows down anyway.

- Carry cash (and maybe one credit card) in a concealed pocket. Strap-on travelers zip pouches work well, too. Dive shops often carry various sized water-proof containers in case you'd like to keep your money dry while swimming. These can attach to your wrist or bathing suit.

- Consider the value of prescription glasses and sentimental items. They could be stolen by accident and no one would come out ahead. If you absolutely must have prescription glasses to function, it's always a good idea to have a spare along. After all, they may get lost or broken quite easily.

- Be prepared to replace anything essential. Important medicines, for example, can be carried in duplicate (one container in your room, another in the car).

- Hawai'i is not the easiest place on designer fashions, expensive shoes, or other high-end clothing, unless you go to a 'total destination resort and never venture out.

- There's more than one way to have your pocket picked. It doesn't hurt to keep your eye on the rental car agencies themselves. Honest mistakes happen, as do other mishaps. Try to see that they don't list your tank as full, when it's just half-full, or talk you into an unneeded upgrade or insurance that you already have. Inspect the car before leaving, and get them to sign off any dents or scratches.

- Don't sign anything you haven't read carefully. Most credit card companies are getting increasingly reluctant to retrieve your money once you've signed on the dotted line.

- Hotels and restaurants have also been known to make mistakes in their favor. At a large resort we were once charged double for what already seemed like an overpriced dinner.

- Pay attention to policies regarding cancellations of bookings for hotels, boats, cars, and tours – these are tending to become stricter. If you don't show, you get to pay anyway.

TUBEWORMS

Phone Charges

You're all aware of the steep rate often charged by hotels for long distance calls. Be alert for the hotel or condo that charges a rather high fee for local calls. (On Lana'i though ALL calls are long distance since they go by way of Maui).

In Hawai'i some hotels and condos have arrangements with certain carriers so that you must use their own service for long distance. This can involve a hefty charge per call for the condo as well as outrageously high charges from the phone company. We once compared short calls from Hawai'i to California made at the same time of day. Nynex had managed to charge approximately ten times as much as AT&T. Since the calls were made on a phone card, the bill didn't arrive until we were back home making it more difficult to dispute.

If you're making many calls, be sure to ask until you're satisfied you know what's going on. Don't expect the information to be sitting next to the phone.

OFTEN HEARD MYTHS

- **"You'll probably never see a shark."**

  If you snorkel often, you probably will see one occasionally, a reef shark, not a Great White or Tiger Shark. Most sharks aren't interested in you for dinner. If you look at actual statistics, your time is better spent worrying about lightning.

- **"Barracudas are harmless to humans."**

  Perhaps some are quite innocuous, but others have bitten off fingers or hands. The Great Barracuda has been involved in the majority of cases we've read. I wouldn't worry about one that has been hanging out in front of a hotel for years, but I wouldn't crowd them either. I'd be even more cautious about eating one for dinner, because they are a definite, major cause of ciguartera "fish poisoning". They are one of the best tasting fish, though, in our experience. Feeling lucky?

- **"Jewelry attracts barracuda bites."**

  I first heard this rumor from a 12-year-old, and it was later reinforced by numerous books. The idea is that the flash will fool a barracuda into attacking. However, we've never heard of a definite case of a woman losing an ear lobe this way, even though I see people swimming and diving with earrings all the time. The same goes for wedding bands. I keep mine on.

- **"The water in Hawai'i is too cold for comfort."**

  It can be pretty cool, especially late winter, especially if you go in naked; but there is an alternative. Just wear a thin wetsuit and it will feel a lot like the Caribbean. Or you can wait till late summer and give the water a chance to warm up. Don't expect warm water in March.

- **"It rains all the time on the Maui"**
  "Maui is too hot and sunny"
  "It's always windy in Maui"

  On Maui you can have the climate of your choice. Don't believe everything you read in advertising literature (like hotel brochures) regarding perfect weather. It does vary, there are seasons, and location matters. It just depends on your personal preferences. You may hit a patch of rain, but on the west side, it seldom lasts for long. The typical weather report for Wailea is: Tonight–fair; Tomorrow, mostly sunny; for the weekend, sunny except for some upslope clouds in the afternoon. The drama of weather is part of the charm of the tropics – enjoy it as it is, rather than expecting it to be exactly as you want.

- **"Octopuses only come out at night."**

Some types are nocturnal, some not. We've seen lots in Hawai'i quite active during the day. The hard part is spotting them! Pay your dues, look sharp, and you'll see one eventually.

- **"Maui is too crowded and commercial."**

While there is certainly no problem buying a T-shirt in Lahaina or finding sun-worshippers in Ka'anapali, there are plenty of spectacular sites to snorkel that are completely uncrowded. As long as you have a car, it's easy to drive to delightful and secluded locations – usually within half an hour from your hotel or condo. Hiking on Maui can take you completely away from civilization as you know it, but a good map (such as ours) can lead you to some lovely snorkeling sites as well as romantic vistas to enjoy the sunset and the view of neighboring islands.

And for really getting away from it all, try a trip to Lana'i. Pay Trilogy or Navatek to take you there with all the trimmings or enjoy a less expensive, more independent and longer day by taking the Expeditions Ferry from Lahaina.

- **"The food it too expensive."**

Rent a condo, check out the great variety of foods at the local grocery store and dine on Japanese, Korean, Chinese, and Hawai'ian specialties. Also try the hearty Hawai'ian lunch, which is reasonable and won't leave room for a full dinner. Be sure to check out the Kona coffee, local fresh fruits, Maui onions, and ever-popular bakeries and ice cream vendors.

BLUESTRIPE BUTTERFLYFISH

SNORKELING THE INTERNET

VISIT OUR WEB PAGE FOR THE LATEST INFO

http://www.wp.com/snorkel_hawaii

The Internet is changing the way we communicate and gather information. Just because you're laid back while you're snorkeling doesn't mean you have to be out of touch with the latest information.

We figure some of you are really wired. You probably brought your laptop along to poolside just for fun. Maybe you don't even have to get out of the water to log on the net, who knows?

We like speed, too, but book writing and publishing is still a slow business. You wouldn't believe how many long, hard hours we spend slaving away, snorkeling and researching, researching and snorkeling some more, in order to produce the little volume you're holding. Maybe a hundred hours of research gets distilled into one little page of maps and text. It makes me sweat just to think about it.

Oh, yeah, some tough job, I hear someone saying. Some folks say that they get no respect; well, we get no sympathy. But we have learned to live with that, and we snorkel on.

To enable you to get the latest corrections and additions between revisions, we have set up a Web page for your benefit. Pull down that left-most menu on your Web browser, and select 'Open Location', or whatever command your browser uses to send you where you want to go. Type in our web site location:

http://www.wp.com/snorkel_hawaii

Hit Enter, and you're there in a flash. We have posted many links to Hawai'ian resources on the World Wide Web (WWW), as well as updates to phone numbers, excursions, and many other goodies. There really are a lot of good resources on the Web, and there are more every day. Check it out!

Check out our progress on other snorkeling guidebooks via our web site. Or you can find out just how to order copies to send to all your friends. A great Christmas or birthday gift, a lot better than another pair of socks for good old Dad! You can even e-mail us using:

indigo@malinowski.com

We'd love to hear what you like or don't like about our books, as well as reports about your experiences snorkeling. If you've found a great snorkeling site anywhere in the world, let us know via e-mail if you can and we'll share some of our favorites, too. The Web is changing hourly, so the best way to get current links is to go to our Web page, and just click on them!

Caveat Surfer

The Web is getting more commercial every day, even though everyone swears no one has figured out how to make money there. It's a libertarian's dream, anarchic, free and open, unfettered and chaotic. There is a downside to unregulated utopias, and it is that you can't tell whether someone has a hidden agenda, knows what they're talking about, or is just plain lying. Things are just not necessarily what they seem on the World Wide Web. Watch out!

Remember to keep a healthy skepticism always with you as you surf the web. Many of the elaborate sites are commercial (is that a shock?), so what seems to be an objective review might just have been bought and paid for. If someone is selling excursions, they may only list those that give them a big cut.

Here are a few Hawai'ian links that may be helpful, and hopefully haven't moved or changed already:

Maui News. Shows current Hawai'ian time. Local news and links.
http://www.mauinews.com/

Virtually Hawaii. Geology-oriented virtual tours. Lots of pictures
http://hawaii.ivv.nasa.gov/space/hawaii/virtual.field.trips.html

Snorkeling areas and tips, courtesy Auntie Snorkel
http://www.maui.net/~travel/snorkel/areas.html

Maui Beaches. Attractive beaches guide, with lots of pictures
http://www.yver.com/~tkern/beaches.html

Hawai'ian Visitors Bureau. Good looking page with lots of links.
http://www.visit.hawaii.org/

Maui Weather Today. Live video, satellite links, great weather info
http://satftp.soest.hawaii.edu/weather/

University of Hawai'i Meteorology Weather Server.
http://lumahai.soest.hawaii.edu/

Hawai'ian kids e-zine. Cute and interactive
http://www.cyber-hawaii.com/aloha/

Native Tongue, Hawai'ian language page. Read, learn and listen, too.
http://www.aloha-hawaii.com/a_speaking.html

INDEX

ABOUT THE AUTHORS

Judy and Mel Malinowski love to snorkel.

They have sought out great snorkeling and cultural experiences since the 70's, traveling to 50-some countries from Anguilla to Zanzibar in the process. Hawai'i keeps drawing them back, and eventually they may become kama'aina.

Although they are certified Scuba divers, the lightness and freedom of snorkeling keeps it their favorite recreation. They also enjoy surface diving, sailing and windsurfing.

Mel, Judy and their three children have hosted students and cultural exchange visitors from Bosnia, Brazil, China, Germany, Nepal, New Zealand, Serbia, and Turkey in their home, and helped hundreds of other families enrich their lives through cultural exchange.

Working with exchange students and traveling as much as their businesses allow has encouraged their interest in the study of languages, from Spanish to Thai and Chinese.

Graduates of Stanford University, they live and work in Palo Alto, California.

ORDER FORM

Indigo
Publications
920 Los Robles Avenue
Palo Alto, CA 94306

Please send _____ copies of *Snorkel Hawai'i: Maui and Lana'i*

_____ copies of *Snorkel Hawai'i: The Big Island*

I have enclosed a check for the full amount, including shipping

Price:	$14.95 per copy CA residents add local sales tax
Shipping:	$2.35 per order by Priority Mail $10.50 Next day air in the USA up to two copies
Special offer:	Order both books together for $24.95 per set Shipping as above

Mail orders:	Send a copy of this form along with your payment to: **Indigo Publications 920 Los Robles Avenue Palo Alto, CA 94306-3127**
Fax:	(415) 493-3642
E-mail:	indigo@malinowski.com

Ship to:

Print or type
clearly, as
this will be
your shipping
label

160